BY FAITH ABEL OFFERED GOD SACRIFICES

A MIXTURE OF HISTORICAL FICTION WITH HISTORICAL NARRATIVE
BASED ON GOD'S WORD

HEROES OF FAITH

ABEL OFFERED ACCEPTABLE SACRIFICES TO GOD

EDWARD D. ANDREWS

EDWARD D. ANDREWS

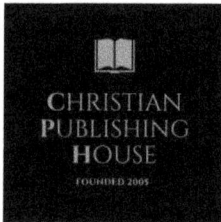

HEROES OF FAITH

Abel Offered Acceptable Sacrifices to God

Edward D. Andrews

Christian Publishing House

Cambridge, Ohio

CHRISTIAN
PUBLISHING
HOUSE
FOUNDED 2005

Christian Publishing House

Professional Conservative Christian
Publishing of the Good News!

CPH Since 2005

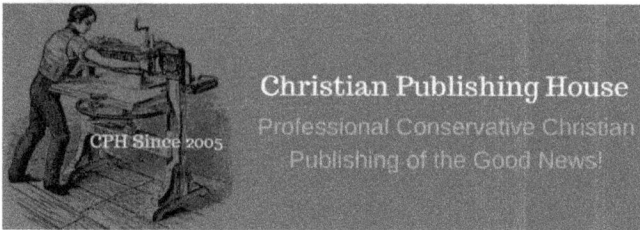

HEROES OF FAITH: Abel Offered Acceptable Sacrifices to God by Edward D. Andrews

ISBN-13: **978-1-949586-06-0**

ISBN-10: **1-949586-06-5**

EDWARD D. ANDREWS

Table of Contents

PREFACE 8

INTRODUCTION What Is Faith 9

    Heroes of Faith (11:1–40) 11

    What Faith Is 11

    Faith and the Men of Old 17

    The Faith of the Patriarchs 21

    The Godly Devotion of the Patriarchs......................... 27

    Faith Moves Us to Put God First 30

ABEL 33

    Living at the Foundation of the World......................... 33

    Abel Develops His Faith.. 34

    A Martyr.. 37

    A Type.. 37

    The Superiority of His Offering................................... 37

Bible Difficulties Answered Surrounding Adam and Eve and Cain and Abel 41

    Genesis 1:27 BDC: Were Adam and Eve Allegorical or Historical Persons?... 42

    Genesis 2:17 BDC: Why did Adam and Eve not die in the day that they ate of the fruit from the forbidden tree? 49

    GENESIS 3:5 OTBDC: Is man made in the image of God or does he become like God?... 52

    GENESIS 3:5 OTBDC: What Was the Original Sin of Adam and Eve? 53

    Genesis 3:8 BDC: Did God speak directly to Adam? 59

    GENESIS 3:16 OTBDC: Are women cursed by God? 61

    GENESIS 3:17 OTBDC: How is it that the ground would be cursed for Adam, and for how long? 63

    Genesis 3:19-21 BDC: Will Adam and Eve Receive a Resurrection? 64

EDWARD D. ANDREWS

Genesis 4:3-4 BDC: Why was Cain's offering unacceptable to God? 66

GENESIS 3:24 OTBDC: Why Has God Permitted Wickedness and Suffering? 69

Genesis 4:8, 12-13 BDC: Why did Cain not receive capital punishment for the murder he committed? 78

GENESIS 4:15 OTBDC: How did God "put a mark on Cain"? 80

Genesis 4:17 OTBDC: Where did Cain get his wife? 82

GENESIS 4:26 OTBDC: Exactly when did the worship of God begin? 84

How Could Satan, Adam, and Eve Have Sinned If They Were Perfect? 85

View of Bible Difficulties **88**

Turning the Tables 90

Some Types of Bible Difficulties **94**

The Text from which our English Bible was Translated 94

Inaccurate Translations 95

False Interpretations of the Bible 96

A Wrong Conception of the Bible 98

The Case of Job 98

The Language in Which the Bible was Written 101

Our Defective Knowledge of the History, Geography and Usages of Bible Times 101

The Ignorance of Conditions under Which Books Were Written and Commands Given 102

The Many-Sidedness of the Bible 103

The Bible has to do with the Infinite, and our Minds are Finite . 104

The Dullness of our Spiritual Perception 104

Dealing With Bible Difficulties **106**

Honestly 106

Humbly 106

Determinedly 106

Fearlessly 106

Patiently...107

Scripturally..107

Prayerfully 107

Bible Difficulties Explained **108**

Inerrancy: Can the Bible Be trusted?........................... 112

Inerrancy: Practical Principles to Overcoming Bible Difficulties .. 117

Inerrancy: Are There Contradictions?.........................124

Inerrancy: Are There Mistakes? 130

Inerrancy: Are There Scientific Errors? 134

Procedures for Handling Biblical Difficulties 137

Bibliography **139**

EDWARD D. ANDREWS

PREFACE

HEROES OF FAITH is historical fiction of the life of the first imperfect human after the fall, Abel, based on the Word of God. After reading the account, it will be as if Abel were an old friend. This brief powerful story will move and motivate the faith of all readers. HEROES OF FAITH has been created to not only entertain but also help the reader strengthen his or her faith. We will begin with an easy to understand introductory chapter on the question, What Is Faith? After that, is the historical story of the life of Abel. This is followed by the Bible difficulties of all Bible person's in the life of Abel: his father Adam, his mother Eve, and his brother Cain. Finally, we close this crucial book that can strengthen us in these last days with four chapters on Bible Difficulties, which will also help the reader grow in faith.

INTRODUCTION What Is Faith

Hebrews 12:1 Updated American Standard Version (UASV)

12 Therefore, since we have so great a cloud of witnesses surrounding us, let us also lay aside every weight and the sin which so easily entangles us, and **let us run with endurance the race** that is set before us,

We might think of a runner in an Olympic race, say the 100 meters, or 100-meter dash. The current men's world record is 9.58 seconds, set by Jamaica's Usain Bolt in 2009 while the women's world record of 10.49 seconds set by American Florence Griffith-Joyner in 1988 remains unbroken. The reigning 100 m Olympic champion is often named "the fastest man in the world." Then, there are the 10,000 meters, which is the longest standard track event. The international distance is equal to approximately 6.2137 miles. Kenenisa Bekele is the current 10,000 m world record holder, 26:17.53. We think of the strain and stress on every fiber of their body whether it be for the quick 100-meter dash or the long 10,000 m marathon.

What about the figurative Christian runner that Paul spoke of in the above text, how does this correlate? They are running in the race of life. We might compare the Olympic 100-meter runner to a Christian making it through each and every day while the 10,000-meter marathon runner to a Christian running his entire life. John Macarthur writes, "The deceased people of [Hebrews] chapter 11 give witness to the value and blessing of living by faith. The motivation for running "the race" is not in the possibility of receiving praise from 'observing' heavenly saints. Rather, the runner is inspired by the godly examples those saints set during their lives. The great crowd is not comprised of spectators but rather is made up of ones whose past life of faith encourages others to live that way (cf. 11:2, 4, 5, 33, 39). **let us.** The reference is to those Hebrews who had made a profession of Christ but had not gone all the way to full faith. They had not yet begun the race, which starts with salvation. The writer has invited them to accept salvation in Christ and join the race. **every weight.** Different from the "sin" mentioned next, this refers to the main encumbrance weighing down the Hebrews, which was the Levitical system with its stifling legalism. The athlete would strip away every piece of unnecessary clothing before competing in the race. The outward things emphasized by the Levitical system not only impede; they also "ensnare." **sin.** In this context, this focuses first on the particular sin of unbelief, refusing to turn away from the Levitical sacrifices to the perfect sacrifice, Jesus Christ (cf. John 16:8–11), as well as other sins cherished by the unbeliever. **endurance.** Endurance is the steady determination to keep going, regardless of the temptation to slow down or give up (cf. 1 Cor. 9:24, 25). **race.** The athletic metaphor presents the faith-filled life as a demanding, grueling effort. The English word agony is derived from the Greek word used here."[1]

Reflecting on the Bible background of Hebrews 12:1, Clinton E. Arnold has, "**IT DOES NOT TAKE LONG EXPERIENCE** in the Christian faith to learn that maintaining a resolute commitment to Christ is not easy and demands endurance. We can find help, however, from several directions. The "cloud of witnesses" reminds us that God's people of the past have walked similar paths as the ones we are walking presently and have done so keeping faith. The exhortation of Scripture to put off those things that hinder us reminds us that the weights we embrace in life—whether unwholesome activities or attitudes of questionable value—can impede our progress in the faith. Finally, we must look to Jesus as the ultimate example of endurance. His attitude of scorning shame gives us a powerful reference point from which to evaluate the difficulties of life, especially those that come because we are committed to God's path." He goes on to write, "So too the author of Hebrews challenges his readers to 'strip' off everything that hinders them in the race of endurance. An ancient writer could use the term *onkos*, translated in 12:1 as [something] 'that hinders,' to refer to a mass, weight, or bodily fat. In the context of running, it could refer to burdensome clothing or excess bodily weight. Therefore, believers are to run the Christian race with endurance, laying aside those things that bind or weigh us down."[2]

The apostle Paul may have had the figurative runners of a race in a stadium in mind when he penned the book of Hebrews for the Jewish Christians in Jerusalem (c. 61 C.E.).[3] The Jewish people were heading into their great tribulation in 66-70 C.E. when the Roman was to come and destroy Jerusalem, so they need firm faith. (Heb. 10:32-39) It would only be by faith that they would heed the prophetic warning of Jesus and flee Jerusalem in 66 C.E., a few short years before to would be destroyed (70 C.E.), wherein over one million Christians were executed by being impaled on a stake and over one hundred thousand were taken back to Rome to be sold as slaves. Faith would also sustain them when they were "who are persecuted for righteousness' sake." – Matthew 5:10; Luke 21:20-24.

---

[1] MacArthur, John (2005-05-09). *The MacArthur Bible Commentary* (Kindle Locations 62741-62752). Thomas Nelson. Kindle Edition.

[2] (Arnold, Zondervan Illustrated Bible Backgrounds Commentary Volume 4: Hebrews to Revelation 2002, p. 75)

[3] B.C.E. means "before the Common Era," which is more accurate than B.C. ("before Christ"). C.E. denotes "Common Era," often called A.D., for *anno Domini*, meaning "in the year of our Lord."

In Hebrews chapter 11 Paul reviewed great persons of faith who lived centuries, even millenniums before the Christian era. He then urged in Hebrews 12:1, "Therefore, since we have so great a cloud of witnesses surrounding us, let us also lay aside every weight [that would hinder us spiritually] and the sin [lack of faith], which so easily entangles us, and let us run with endurance the race [for life eternal] that is set before us." Paul's review of faith highlighted several facets of it and will help us as well today. The question that might seem obvious to some is, "what is faith?" What are the specific aspects that can be beneficial to us? First, Bible scholar David S. Dockery will give us an overview of Hebrews chapter 11.

Heroes of Faith (11:1-40)

As an incentive to endurance before God, the writer presented a gallery of Old Testament heroes of faith. Faith gives reality to things that cannot be seen. By this faith, the Old Testament believers received a positive witness from God. In the generations before the flood, Abel, Enoch, and Noah all responded by faith to demonstrate obedience to God. Their faith pleased Him. Abraham demonstrated his faith by forsaking the comforts of Ur and Haran to follow God to the promised land. By faith Abraham and Sarah bore Isaac as a child of their old age. Moses showed his faith by leaving the wealth of the Egyptian palace to suffer hardship with the Hebrew people. The writer presented Gideon, Samson, David, Samuel, and many other heroes as examples whose faith Christians should follow. The promises the Old Testament believers had expected were coming true in the events New Testament Christians were experiencing.[4]

What Faith Is

Hebrews 11:1-3 Updated American Standard Version (UASV)

11 Now faith is the assurance[5] of things hoped for, the conviction[6] of things not seen. **2** For by means of it, the men of old[7] had witness borne to them. **3** By faith we understand that the worlds[8] were prepared by the word of God, so that what is seen was not made out of things which are visible.

---

[4] (D. S. Dockery, HOLMAN CONCISE BIBLE COMMENTARY Simple, straightforward commentary on every book of the Bible 1998, p. 625)

[5] Lit *a sub-standing*; Gr *hypostasis*

[6] Or *convincing evidence*

[7] Or *of ancient times*; Lit *older men*; Gr *presbyteroi*.

[8] Or *universe*; Lit *ages*

The apostle Paul defined faith as "the assurance[9] of things hoped for." The one who has faith has an absolute guarantee that everything God says will come to pass, will be fulfilled. Faith is also, "the conviction[10] of things not seen." The convincing evidence of the unseen is so powerful that faith is viewed as being the same as that evidence.[11]

By means of faith, "the men of old[12] had witness borne to them" that they had a righteous standing before God. In addition, "by faith we understand that the worlds[13] [earth, the sun, the moon, and the stars] were prepared by the word of God," "so that what is seen was not made out of things which are visible." (Gen. 1:1; John 4:24; Rom. 1:20) Below, we will let several different leading Bible scholars address Hebrews 11:1-3, as it is the foundation of this book. We will begin with the author that is easiest to understand and work our way to the more difficult, so by the time we get to the more difficult we have the basic knowledge, to grasp the deeper things.

Faith

On Hebrews 11:1-3, William Barclay writes, "TO the writer to the Hebrews, faith is a hope that is absolutely certain that what it believes is true and that what it expects will come. It is not the hope which looks forward with wistful longing; it is the hope which looks forward with utter conviction. In the early days of persecution, a humble Christian was brought before the judges. He told them that nothing they could do could shake him because he believed that, if he was true to God, God would be true to him. 'Do you really think,' asked the judge, 'that the likes of you will go to God and his glory?' 'I do not think,' said the man, 'I know.' At one time, John Bunyan was tortured by uncertainty. 'Everyone doth think his own Religion rightest,' he said, 'both Jews and Moors and Pagans; and how if all our Faith and Christ and Scriptures should be but a "Think so" too?' But, when the light broke, he ran out crying: 'Now I know! I know!' The Christian faith is a hope that has turned to certainty. This Christian hope is such that it dictates every aspect of the way Christians conduct

---

[9] Lit *a sub-standing*; Gr *hypostasis*

[10] Or *convincing evidence*

[11] "This verse is written in a style of Hebrew poetry (used often in the Psalms), in which two parallel and nearly identical phrases are used to state the same thing. Cf. 1 Peter 1:7— God tests our faith in the crucible. **Substance.** This is from the same Greek word translated "express image" in 1:3 and 'confidence' in 3:14. The faith described here involves the most solid possible conviction, the God-given present assurance of a future reality. **evidence of things not seen.** True faith is not based on empirical evidence but on divine assurance and is a gift of God (Eph. 2:8)." – MacArthur, John (2005-05-09). *The MacArthur Bible Commentary* (Kindle Locations 62577-62581). Thomas Nelson. Kindle Edition.

[12] Or *of ancient times*; Lit *older men*; Gr *presbyteroi*.

[13] Or *universe*; Lit *ages*

themselves. They live in it and they die in it; and it is the possession of it which makes them act as they do."[14]

On Hebrews 11:1-3, Thomas D. Lea writes, "**11:1.** Eyesight produces a conviction about objects in the physical world. Faith produces the same convictions for the invisible order. Faith shows itself by producing assurance that what we hope for will happen. Faith also provides an insight into realities which otherwise remain unseen. A person with faith lets these unseen realities from God provide a living, effective power for daily life. **11:2–3.** These verses present two illustrations of the use of faith. First, faith enabled the heroes of the Old Testament to receive a good standing with God. God gave his approval to the faith of these saints. Second, believing that God created the world involves a leap of faith. Faith points to an unseen power who made the world we see. The **universe** involves more than the physical world. It includes the ages that God had planned, beginning with the act of creation and extending to the consummation of all things in Christ. By faith, we know that all we see around us and all that takes place on earth came from one we cannot see. By observing creation we may learn of God's power. We learn the manner of God's creation only by responding in faith to the statements of Scripture." (T. D. Lea, Holman New Testament Commentary: Hebrews, James 1999, p. 201)

On Hebrews 11:1-3, Simon J. Kistemaker writes, "The heroes of faith have one thing in common: they put their undivided confidence in God. In spite of all their trials and difficult circumstances, they triumphed because of their trust in God. For the author, faith is adhering to the promises of God, depending on the Word of God, and remaining faithful to the Son of God. When we see chapter 11 in the context of Hebrews, the author's design to contrast faith with the sin of unbelief (3:12,19; 4:2; 10:38–39) becomes clear. Over against the sin of falling away from the living God, the writer squarely places the virtue of faith.[15] Those people who shrink from putting their trust in God are destroyed, but those who believe are saved (10:39)."[16]

Assurance

Kistemaker goes on, "The author of Hebrews expresses that same assurance in much more concise wording: "Faith is being sure of what we hope for." The expression *being sure* of is given as 'substance' in other translations. The difference between these translations arises from understanding the original Greek word *hypostasis* subjectively or

---

[14] *Barclay, William (2010-11-05). The Letter to the Hebrews (New Daily Study Bible) (pp. 152-153). Westminster John Knox Press. Kindle Edition.*

[15] F. W. Grosheide, *De Brief aan de Hebreeën en de Brief van Jakobus* (Kampen: Kok. 1955), p. 255.

[16] (S. J. Kistemaker, Baker New Testament Commentary: Hebrews 1984, P. 310)

objectively. If I am sure of something, I have certainty in my heart. This is a subjective knowledge because it is within me. Assurance, then, is a subjective quality. By contrast, the word *substance* is objective because it refers to something that is not part of me. Rather, substance is something on which I can rely. As one translation has it, 'Faith is the title-deed of things hoped for.'[17] That, in fact, is objective."

He goes on, "To come to a clear-cut choice in the matter is not easy, for the one translation does not rule out the other. The translation *confidence* or *assurance* has gained prominence, perhaps because 3:14 also has the same word: "We have come to share in Christ if we hold firmly till the end the confidence we had at first." In the case of 11:1, even though the objective sense has validity, the subjective meaning is commended."

Kistemaker concludes "The author [Paul] teaches the virtue of hope wherever he can introduce the topic (3:6; 6:11, 18; 7:19; 10:23). Hope is not an inactive hidden quality. Hope is active and progressive. It relates to all the things God has promised to believers: "all things of present grace and future glory."[18] (S. J. Kistemaker, Baker New Testament Commentary: Hebrews 1984, P. 311)

Certainty

Faith

is

being sure of	certain of
what we hope for	what we do not see

Kistemaker writes, "In short, assurance is balanced by certainty. These two nouns are in this text synonymous. Certainty, then, means 'inner conviction.'[19] The believer is convinced that the things he is unable to see are real. Not every conviction, however, is equal to faith. Conviction is the equivalent of faith when certainty prevails, even though the evidence is lacking. The things we do not see are those that pertain to the future that in time will become the present. Even things of the present, and certainly those of the past, that are beyond our reach belong to the category of 'what we do not see.' Comments B. F. Westcott, 'Hope includes that which is

[17] James Hope Moulton and George Milligan, *The Vocabulary of the Greek Testament Illustrated from the Papyri and Other Non-Literary Sources* (London: Hodder and Stoughton, 1930), pp.659–60.
[18] John Owen, *An Exposition of Hebrews*, 7 vols. in 4 (Evansville, Ind.: Sovereign Grace, 1960), vol. 7, p. 7.
[19] Bauer, p. 249.

internal as well as that which is external.'[20] Hope centers in the mind and spirit of man; sight relates to one of his senses (Rom. 8:24–25). Faith, therefore, radiates from man's inner being where hope resides to riches that are beyond his purview. Faith demonstrates itself in confident assurance and convincing certainty."[21]

Some Christians who claim to have faith are confusing it with a somewhat, easygoing, good-natured sentimentality, a more or less 'faith in faith.' These ones feel that they believe in God, so they emotionally know that God exists. However, to be honest, this lukewarm faith will have little effect on their life when tragedy strikes. Therefore, faith-based on emotions is impractical, although it will seem quite real until difficult times befall them.

However, the genuine, true faith that the Bible encourages is very different. It is "the assurance[22] of things hoped for, the conviction[23] of things not seen." – Hebrews 11:1.

The Greek word behind our English translation "assurance" (*hypostasis*) carries the idea of something that lies beneath or guarantees what is expected. Therefore, this Biblical faith is not some meager, emotional, ambiguous feeling or an unsupported hope; real assurance is involved. The Greek word behind our English translation "conviction" (*elenchos*) carries the thought of presenting convincing evidence (literally, the proof) particularly evidence that establishes something other than what many might believe to be so. This is evidence that moves someone to agree fully, understand, and grasp the truth or soundness of something; especially based on argument or discussion. Accordingly, even though we live in a world filled with people who say there is no God; our faith in him comes not from emotionalism, but rather convincing evidence.

Where are we on this? Can we say that we have assurance, maintained by convincing evidence that God exists?

Faith Is the Evidence of Things Not Seen

The definition of faith continues: "faith is ... the evidence of things not seen." The author uses a reference to one of the senses of the human body through which we gain knowledge, the sense of sight. There is a popular expression today, "Seeing is believing." Similarly, people from Missouri like to say, "Show me." This attitude is not opposed to biblical faith, for the New Testament calls us to put our trust in the gospel not

---

[20] B. F. Westcott, *Commentary on the Epistle to the Hebrews* (Grand Rapids: Eerdmans, 1950), p. 350.

[21] (S. J. Kistemaker, Baker New Testament Commentary: Hebrews 1984, P. 311)

[22] Lit *a sub-standing*; Gr *hypostasis*

[23] Or *convincing evidence*

on the basis of some irrational leap into the darkness but on the basis of the testimony of eyewitnesses who report in Scripture about what they saw.

Think, for example, of the apostolic testimony of Peter: "For we did not follow cleverly devised myths when we made known to you the power and coming of our Lord Jesus Christ, but we were eyewitnesses of his majesty" (2 Peter 1:16). Likewise, when Luke begins his Gospel, he addresses it to Theophilus, saying, "it seemed good to me ..., having followed all things closely for some time past, to write an orderly account for you" (v. 3). He is talking about things he has substantiated on the basis of eyewitness testimony. In the same way, when Paul defends his confidence in the resurrection in 1 Corinthians 15, he appeals to the eyewitnesses of the risen Christ: Cephas, the Twelve, the five hundred, James, and all the apostles (vv. 5–7). Then he writes, "Last of all, as to one untimely born, he appeared also to me" (v. 8). Paul is saying, "I believe in the resurrection because many eyewitnesses saw the resurrected Christ, and I saw Him myself."

So there is a link in the New Testament between faith and seeing, and yet the author of Hebrews describes faith as the conviction of things *not* seen. Maybe this is why some people argue that there is a biblical ground for regarding blind faith as virtuous. After all, if one cannot see, one is said to be blind, so if faith is evidence for that which cannot be seen, that must mean that the faith of which the author is speaking is blind faith.

I cannot think of anything that is farther from the meaning of Hebrews 11:1–2 than blind faith. Those promoting blind faith say: "We believe what we believe for no reason whatsoever. It's totally gratuitous." The idea is that there's some kind of virtue in closing our eyes, taking a deep breath, and wishing with all of our might that something is true—then saying, "It's true." That is credulity, not faith.

The Bible never claims that we should jump into the darkness. In fact, the biblical injunction is for people to come out of the darkness and into the light (cf. John 3:19). Faith is not blind in the sense of being arbitrary, whimsical, or a mere expression of human desire. If that were the case, why would the author of Hebrews say that faith is "the evidence of things not seen"?

When faith is linked to hope, it is put into the time frame of the future, and the one thing that I cannot see at all is tomorrow. None of us has yet experienced tomorrow. As I said earlier, I have hope that the Pittsburgh Steelers will win their football games. But I cannot know in advance whether that will happen or not.

However, Hebrews says that faith is the *evidence* of things not seen. Evidence is tangible. Evidence is something we can know through our five senses. Evidence is what police officers inspect and try to collect at a crime scene—fingerprints, traces of gunpowder residue, articles of clothing that are left behind, and so on. All these things are visible and point beyond themselves to some important truth. That's why people analyze evidence.

The idea is this: I don't know what tomorrow is going to bring, but I know that God knows what tomorrow is going to bring. So if God promises that tomorrow will bring something, and if I trust God for tomorrow, I have faith in something I have not yet seen. That faith serves as evidence because its object is God. I know Him; He has a track record—He is infallible and never lies. God knows everything and is perfect in whatever He communicates. So if God tells me that something is going to happen tomorrow, I believe it even though I haven't seen it yet.

That's not credulity or irrationality. On the contrary, it is irrational *not* to believe something that God says regarding some future event.

What does God say regarding the future? He not only reveals to us events of tomorrow that we haven't yet seen, He also reveals to us much about the supernatural realm that our eyes cannot penetrate. We cannot see angels at this time. We cannot see heaven. But God reveals to us the reality of these things, and by faith we see that they have substance because God is credible. (Sproul 2010, pp. 5-8)

Faith and the Men of Old

Hebrews 11:4 Updated American Standard Version (UASV)

[4] By faith Abel offered to God a better sacrifice than Cain, through which he obtained the testimony that he was righteous, God testifying about his gifts, and through faith,[24] though he is dead, he still speaks.

There are two aspects of Cain's offering, which found him unapproved before God: **(1)** his attitude and **(2)** the type of offering.

It seems that Abel, the second born of Adam and Eve, was capable of discerning the need for blood to be involved in the atoning sacrifice, while Cain was not, or simply did not care. Therefore, it was the heart attitude of Cain that resulted in his sacrifice being rejected. Consequently, "but on Cain and his offering, he did not look with favor. So Cain was very angry, and his face was downcast." (Gen 4:5, NIV) It may well be that Cain had little regard for the atoning sacrifice, giving it little thought, going through the motions of the act only. However, as later biblical history would show, God is not one to be satisfied with formal worship. Cain had developed a bad heart attitude, and God well knew that his motives were not sincere.

---

[24] Lit *it*

The way Cain reacted to the evaluation of his sacrifice only evidenced what God already knew. Instead of seeking to improve the situation, 'Cain grew very angry.'

One of the many aspects of faith is our understanding and appreciating that there is a need for a sacrifice for sins. Just after Adam and Eve were expelled from the Garden of Eden, Abel demonstrated faith in a blood sacrifice. Clearly, Abel must have discerned that he had inherited sin (missing the mark of perfection) from his parents. (Gen. 2:16-17; 3:6-7; See Rom. 5:12) Obviously, Abel must have seen the fulfillment of God's decree on Adam, cursing the ground, saying that in pain he would eat of it as growing food would be very difficult. God concluded, "By the sweat of your face you shall eat bread, till you return to the ground, for out of it you were taken; for you are dust, and to dust you shall return." (Gen 3:17-19) He must have also been aware of the fulfillment of God's decree on Eve, "I will surely multiply your pain in childbearing; in pain you shall bring forth children. Your desire shall be for your husband, and he shall rule over you." (Gen. 3:16, ESV) Therefore, Abel had "the assurance of" God's word coming true. (Heb. 11:1) This would include the prophetic word concerning Satan the Devil, who had projected his voice through the serpent in Eden, contributing to the rebellion of Adam and Eve. God said to the serpent, i.e., Satan, "I will put enmity between you and the woman, and between your offspring and her offspring; he shall bruise your head, and you shall bruise his heel." – Genesis 3:15.

Abel demonstrated his faith in the promised seed spoken of By God by his discerning the need to offer up an animal sacrifice, which could substitute for Abel's blood, though not completely. However, Cain and his bloodless vegetables evidenced a lack of faith or a failure to understand. Moreover, his attitude showed that he really did not care to understand. (Genesis 4:1-8) As Abel struggled for his life, he could know that he had a righteous standing before God,[25] as Paul said, "God testifying about his gifts." How did God testify about Abel's gifts? The Father accepted Abel's sacrifices that he offered in faith. Clearly, "though he is dead, he still speaks." Can we say that we evidence faith in Jesus Christ's greater ransom sacrifice? – 1 John 2:1-2.

Hebrews 11:5-6 Updated American Standard Version (UASV)

[5] By faith Enoch was transferred[26] so as not to see death, and he was not to be found because God had transferred him; for before he was

---

[25] 1 John 3:23 English Standard Version (ESV)
[23] And this is his commandment, that we believe in the name of his Son Jesus Christ and love one another, just as he has commanded us.

[26] **to convey from one place to another,** *put in another place, transfer* – BDAG, p. 642.

Canaanite idolatry, his wife was barren. But the text only allows one—survival. The people of Canaan realized that Egypt was the bread basket of the world at that time [see "Deeper Discoveries"]. Griffith Thomas criticizes Abram for this decision and adds, "It would certainly seem that Abraham was now thinking solely of the land and its famine, and forgetting God and His promises" (Thomas, 119). Kidner adds, "His craven and tortuous calculations are doubly revealing, both of the natural character of this spiritual giant and of the sudden transition that can be made from the plane of faith to that of fear" (Kidner, 116). But the text never faults Abraham for making the trip, only for lying about Sarai.[30]

Notice the logic in the author's reasoning, "the text never faults Abram for the trip." We will build on this logic, for our setting the record straight about Abraham. Now, notice, in the very next sentence he drops the ball, calling Abraham a liar in the negative sense. He also states that the text faults Abraham for lying about Sarai. This is not true, but rather his reading it into the text. More on that in a moment, as we will now go to number (1), Ur was a place of idol worship in which Abram and his family participated. – Joshua 24:2-14.

Response: Living in the midst of idolatry it is likely that Terah and his family engaged in it idol worship, which is what the text says, "Thus says the Lord, the God of Israel, 'Long ago, your fathers lived beyond the Euphrates, Terah, the father of Abraham and of Nahor; and they served other gods." However, the text says Terah and his family, which would have made up many people, including their slaves. We could be considering dozens of people, if not more. Thus, Abraham is mentioned because he is one of the most prominent persons within Scripture and he is the Son of Terah and the father of the Israelites. The reference "they" of "they served other gods," need not include Abraham.

Moreover, God specifically chose Abraham for his great faith. In fact, the rest of the Scriptures are founded on this man of faith. Faith is not based on simple belief, but rather on knowledge, understanding, and wisdom. Abraham was the only one from the postflood era, who was evidencing faith in God. In addition, it is truly likely that his knowledge, understanding, and wisdom came from a preflood person, i.e., Shem, the son of Noah, the only son to remain faithful. Shem lived 150 years into Abraham's life, meaning that Abraham's first 75 years before leaving Mesopotamia could very well have been personally associated with Shem. (Gen 9:26) Shem lived 500 years after fathering Arpachshad, dying at the age of 600 years.

---

[30] Anders, Max; Gangel, Kenneth; Bramer, Stephen J. (2003-04-01). *Holman Old Testament Commentary - Genesis.* 1 (pp. 121-122). B&H Publishing. Kindle Edition.

(Gen 11:10-11) He actually dies about 13 years after the death of Sarah. Returning to Joshua, the verse reads, "your fathers lived beyond the Euphrates, Terah, the father of Abraham and of Nahor; and **they served other gods.**" Again, the "they" does not have to refer to Abraham just because he is mentioned in the verse. Yes, he is mentioned in the verse, but Terah was the father, the patriarch, and he had a very big family, so it is not as if Joshua could list them all. Abraham was referred to because of his being the most prominent one in Scripture. I say that since it does not out and out, point the finger at Abraham and, when we consider that God explicitly chose Abraham because of his great faith, it is not likely Joshua was including Abraham. Would this be the case if Abraham had been an idol worshiper? No, it is because Abraham displayed great faith in God that he picked him to be the line to the Messiah. He earned the reputation "the righteousness of the faith which he had while uncircumcised, so that he might be the father of all who believe without being circumcised, that righteousness might be credited to them." – Romans 4:11.

What about accusation number **(3)** Abraham lied about his wife Sarai, saying she was his sister when they went into Egypt because he was only concerned about how he would be treated. Now, notice that the Homan commentators again find fault with Abraham. The Holman Commentary has,

> The Bedouin scheme he concocted was to speak a half-truth about his sister-wife. This was a subtle way to salve his own conscience. She was indeed his sister (actually a half-sister; cp. 20:12), so he conveyed to the Egyptians only what he wanted them to know. His motive was undoubtedly based on patriarchal society laws (cp. Laban, 24:29-61). In enemy territory a husband could be killed for his wife. But if Abram were known as her brother, someone wanting her would have to make marriage arrangement with him, which would possibly give him time to react in his own interest" (Ross, 49). 12:14-16. Abram had not counted on Sarai being approached by the one man in Egypt who needed no special permission to take a woman. Abram's selfish concern of verse 13 ["so that I will be treated well"] may have stuck in his throat, for Moses writes of Pharaoh, he treated Abram well. Wealth in the ancient Middle East was not measured in gold but in animals, slaves, and land. 12:17-20. Abram's sin brought God's judgment on Pharaoh's house. But in a true demonstration of biblical grace, God overcame Abram's sin, forgave his lie, and sent him back to the land. Egyptian ethics insisted on absolute truthfulness, so Abram's behavior offended his hosts. Abram probably learned two important spiritual lessons from this side trip to Egypt—truth and trust. The lesson of trust he exemplified

throughout the rest of his life. The issue of truth, unfortunately, gave him difficulty on at least one other occasion.[31]

Response: The standard of God is that there is no lying, which Exodus 20:16 makes all too clear, "You shall not bear false witness against your neighbor." However, When Abram was forced to go down to Egypt, because of a famine, he "said to Sarai his wife, 'I know that you are a woman beautiful in appearance, and when the Egyptians see you, they will say, 'This is his wife.' Then they will kill me, but they will let you live. Say you are my sister, that it may go well with me because of you, and that my life may be spared for your sake.'" (12:12-13) In Genesis chapter 20, we find Abraham repeating this behavior, even though it did not bode well for him the first time. Did Abraham lie these two times, and if so, why does the entire account of Abraham present him as righteously walking with God, the epitome of faith?

First, it should be mentioned that Sarah was the half-sister and wife of Abraham. Therefore, in essence, he did not lie about their relationship; he only withheld information that would have been used by the enemy, resulting in Abraham being possibly killed. It is true malicious lying is prohibited in the Bible, which is to say something that is not true in a conscious effort to deceive or hurt somebody that is deserving of the truth. However, the Bible has examples or cases where a person has withheld information from the enemy, who would have used that information to hurt or cause harm to a person or another. The Bible seems to suggest that we are not under obligation to divulge information to the enemy, which would result in our harm or the harm of another. The American legal system allows something like this as well. It is called The Fifth Amendment (Amendment V), which guarantees you do not have to testify against yourself.

Jesus Christ counseled, "Do not give dogs what is holy, and do not throw your pearls before pigs, lest they trample them underfoot and turn to attack you." (Matt 7:6) Even Jesus himself, who is incapable of malicious lying, on occasion, withheld information from those who were not worthy of it and would have only used it to hurt him. (Matt 15:1-6; 21:23-27; John 7:3-10) We see this same principle underway with Abraham, Isaac, Rehab, and Elisha, as all pointed in the wrong direction or withheld all the facts from the enemies or non-worshipers.[32]

---

[31] Anders, Max; Gangel, Kenneth; Bramer, Stephen J. (2003-04-01). *Holman Old Testament Commentary - Genesis*: 1 (p. 122). B&H Publishing. Kindle Edition.
[32] Genesis 12:10-19; chap 20; 26:1-10; Jos 2:1-6; James 2:25; 2 Kings 6:11-23

- A crazed gunman breaks into our house, and asks you, "Is anyone else here?" Are we obligated to tell him that your two little girls are upstairs hiding under the bed?

- What if we see a woman run into an alley to escape someone who is trying to kill her, and he asks us, "Where is she?" What do we do? Do we send him on a wild goose chase to protect the woman's life? Or do we lead them to him to the victim? – William Lane Craig

- During World War II, we are bringing a food box into a concentration camp. The guard asked us if there is any contraband inside. Would we be obligated to tell him that we have a small Bible smuggled into one of the packages?

- Are we to endanger a human life, or do we withhold information that the enemy does not deserve, nor have the right to, even giving them misinformation?

The advice offered here is twofold: **(1)** Do not read anything into the text that is not clearly stated, especially if it shines a negative light on someone like the father of all having faith, i.e., Abraham. All Scripture is inspired, meaning that the inspired writers of the New Testament can often settle gray areas in the Old Testament. **(2)** If the verse does not say it explicitly but, seems to suggest a negative on the first glance; then, look at the whole book for context, as well as the entire Bible. If it is a man or woman that God had special dealings with, give them the benefit of the doubt. If it is a person like wicked Nimrod; then, we can suggest such things. Use the entire Bible, as it is one book, by one author, with 40 plus writers, who wrote under inspiration, being led along by Holy Spirit. Again, many commentators tend to project unnecessary negative perceptions of Bible characters when the Bible itself has them in a positive light. Readers should ignore this. – **End of Excursion**

The wives of the patriarchs, Sarah, Rebekah, and Rachel also had faith in God's promises. Many times, we tend to overlook the faithful women of Scripture. Scripture encourages us to 'consider the outcome of faithful one's way of life and imitate their faith.' It also says, 'be imitators of those who through faith and patience inherit the promises. Dear Christian sisters; imagine what it would be like to have been neighbors, even friends with Rachel, Rebekah, Ruth, Hannah, Abigail, Esther, Mary, and the like. How might have they affected your life? For example, by faith Sarah, who had been barren for 90 years, "received power to conceive, even when she was past the age since she considered him [God] faithful who had promised." Soon enough, Sarah gave birth to Isaac. Therefore, Abraham, who was one hundred at the time, "who was as good as dead in these things [reproduction]," had "as many descendants as the stars of heaven in number and as innumerable as the sand by the seashore." – Genesis 17:15-17; 18:11; 21:1-7.

EXCURSION Understanding Abraham and Sarah's Laughter (Genesis 17:17-18; 18:9-15)

Both Abraham and Sarah laughed when the angel announced that, they were to have a son when Abraham was 100 years old, and Sarah was 90. (Gen 18:16–21:7) We can note from the account that Abraham was **not** rebuked for his laughing, but Sarah was, which she even tried to deny. Therefore, there is no reason to see Abraham's laughter as nothing more than that of joy, for he was finally going to have a son with his beloved Sarah. However, Sarah's laughter was something more, as she saw this amazing prospect as humorous. In other words, the idea of having a child at the age of 90, when she had been barren all these years, struck her as funny. Maybe she was picturing her 90-year-old body being nine months pregnant and what she would have looked like. However, no one can rightfully look at the account, and come away with either Abraham or Sarah laughing because of contempt, disrespect or deliberate sarcasm as both are recorded as demonstrating faith in the promise God made. (Rom 4:18-22; Heb. 11:1, 8-12) – **End of Excursion**

The Godly Devotion of the Patriarchs

Hebrews 11:13-16 Updated American Standard Version (UASV)

[13] These all died in faith, not having received the things promised, but having seen them and greeted them from afar, and having acknowledged that they were strangers and temporary residents in the land.[33] [14] For those who say such things make it clear that they are seeking a home territory of their own. [15] And indeed if they had been thinking of that territory from which they went out, they would have had opportunity to return. [16] But as it is, they desire a better territory, that is, a heavenly one.[34] Therefore God is not ashamed to be called their God, for he has prepared for them a city.

Faith will help us to remain devoted to God even when we do not even see the fulfillment of his promises. The patriarchs were promised that the new land (Canaan) would be theirs, and they would have descendants that outnumbered the stars or the sands of the seashore, yet they died without seeing that promise fulfilled. However, they saw [the promises]

---

[33] Lit on the earth; the Greek (*ges*) literally means "earth, land, region, humanity," and it is the context that determines our word choice. The Greek here means the surface of the earth as the habitation of humanity. (BDAG) Dods and Lane, take it in reference to the land of Canaan. (Dods, "Hebrews," 357; Lane, *Hebrews 9–13*, 357) See vs 16 note

[34] The patriarchs were not looking for any spiritual, heavenly resurrection

"from afar, and having acknowledged that they were strangers and temporary residents in the land." Yes, they faithfully lived very long lives in tough times, as they faced life and death, for centuries would pass before future generations would take possession of the Promised Land.

EXCURSION "in the land" vs "on the earth" and "a heavenly one"

It can be a bit misleading if the text is translated literally in verse 13, "on the earth," as opposed to interpretively, "in the land." This is especially so when verse 16 says the patriarchs were looking for a better 'land' or 'territory,' namely a heavenly one.' These texts could cause the reader to believe that the patriarchs were looking for some spiritual, heavenly kingdom.

Abraham and his family left Ur of the Chaldeans, and he no longer wanted that city. If the patriarchs had been "thinking of that territory from which they went out [Ur of the Chaldeans], they would have had opportunity to return." Abraham and his son Isaac, as well as his grandson Jacob and his great-grandson Joseph 'desired a better territory,' that is, "a heavenly one," i.e., they looked for a heavenly like territory prepared by God. Bible commentators Dods and Lane, take it in reference to the land of Canaan, i.e., the Promised Land, which was described as being like the Garden of Eden.[35] It should be added that Jerusalem was the "city of our God" (Psa. 46:4; 48:1, 8; 87:3; Heb. 12:22) and the city of Jehovah (Psa. 48:8; 101:8; Isa. 60:14, ASV), its name means "two-fold peace." The things promised to these patriarchs were possession of the land, the founding of a nation, and blessing that would come from Abraham's offspring. These are the things the patriarchs looked for, which would have been encompassed in the land of Canaan, known as the Promised Land.

In 30 C.E., Jesus told Nicodemus, "No one has ascended into heaven except he who descended from heaven, the Son of Man." (John 3:13) In essence, Jesus said that Abraham, Isaac, and Jacob, nor Joseph, not even David were in heaven. Some three years later, Pentecost 33 C.E., the apostle Peter said similarly, "For David did not ascend into the heavens." If David did not ascend into the heavens, the same would be true of Abraham, Isaac, Jacob, and Joseph. The opportunity for life in heaven was not available to imperfect humans when they died, until the death, resurrection, and ascension of Jesus Christ. (Jn. 14:2-3; Heb. 9:24; 10:19-20) This is why we are told in 2 Kings 2:10, "then David slept with his fathers [he died] and was buried in the city of David." In other words, David had the hope of a future resurrection, once the ransom was paid. (Gen 3:15) The hope of a heavenly resurrection is not discussed in the Old Testament, or any time prior to Christ, as he is the first to bring it up. (Matt.

---

[35] See Num. 13:23; Deut. 8:7-9; 11:9, 11-15; 26:15; Isa. 51:3; 58:11; Jer. 31:12; Eze. 36:35

19:21, 23-28; Lu 12:32; John 14:2-3) The resurrection hope was not fully understood until after Pentecost 33 C.E. (Acts 1:6-8; 2:1-4, 29-36; Rom. 8:16-17) Even Job expected that at his death, he would be asleep in death in the grave, until a future resurrection. (Job 14:13-15) What these patriarchs looked for was a heavenly like city prepared by God. The patriarchs were **not** looking for some spiritual, heavenly kingdom. – **End of Excursion**

Just because the prophetic promises were not fulfilled within their lifetime, this did not embitter Abraham, Isaac, Jacob, and Joseph. This did not cause them to turn away from the only true God. No, they did not take the easy way out by running back to Ur of the Chaldeans, where life was easier, having many relatives that were likely involved in worldly activities.[36] No, those patriarchs "desire a better territory, that is, a heavenly one," namely, looking for a heavenly like territory prepared by God, in the land of Canaan, known as the Promised Land, containing the city of God, Jerusalem. 'Therefore, God is not ashamed to be called their God, for he has prepared for them a city.' They remained faithful until death having a hope of a future resurrection, where the Messiah, Jesus Christ, whom they were never able to see will bring them back. (John 5:28-29; Acts 24:15)[37] What about us, have we been walking with God for some time? We must maintain our confidence in the return of Christ, even if it does not happen in our lifetime. (3 John 1:4; 2 Peter 3:11-13) The reward is well worth anything we might suffer for the faith, and the promises are true.

Hebrews 11:17-19 Updated American Standard Version (UASV)

[17] By faith Abraham, when he was tested, offered up[38] Isaac, and he who had received the promises was offering up[39] his only begotten son, [18] of whom it was said, "In Isaac your seed[40] shall be called," [19] having reasoned that God was able even to raise him from the dead, from which, figuratively speaking,[41] he did receive him back.

One of the most important aspects of genuine faith is unquestioning obedience to God. Since Abraham obeyed God without question, he

---

[36] Compare John 17:16; 2 Timothy 4:10; James 1:27; 1 John 2:15-17.

[37] **Resurrection Hope - Where?** (http://tiny.cc/5uz4sy)

[38] An interpretive translation could read, "as good as offered up Isaac." The Greek verb here (*prosenenochen*) translated "offered up" is in the perfect tense, where the writer describes "a completed verbal action that occurred in the past but which produced a state of being or a result that exists in the present (in relation to the writer). The emphasis of the perfect is not the past action so much as it is as such but the present 'state of affairs' resulting from the past action." (GMSDT) Dods and Moffatt take the perfect tense to refer only to a past act with no emphasis being suggested by the author. (Dods, "Hebrews," 358; Moffatt, Hebrews, 176.)

[39] The Greek verb here (*prosepheren*) translated "was offering up" is in the imperfect tense, "where the writer portrays an action in process or a state of being that is occurring in the past with no assessment of the action's completion." (GMSDT) Therefore, this rendering is in harmony with what actually happened.

[40] Or *descendants; offspring*

[41] Lit *in a parable;* Gr *enparabolei*

offered up Isaac, his only begotten son, i.e., the only one he had by Sarah. How could Abraham have listened to a command to offer Isaac? Because he "reasoned that God was able even to raise him from the dead, from which" the promised offspring would come. Abraham held the knife high above his head ready to plunge it into Isaac, ending his life, when an angel's voice brought him to a halt. Therefore, Abraham received Isaac back from the dead in a figurative way. We too should be ready to obey God even if life is in jeopardy, as there will be a future resurrection. (1 John 5:3) It should be mention that, Abraham and Isaac portrayed how the Father would offer up his only-begotten Son, Jesus Christ, as a ransom sacrifice so that those having faith in him might receive eternal life. – Genesis 22:1-19; John 3:16.

Hebrews 11:20-22 Updated American Standard Version (UASV)

22 By faith also Isaac blessed Jacob and Esau concerning things to come. 21 By faith Jacob, as he was dying, blessed each of the sons of Joseph, and worshiped, leaning on the top of his staff. 22 By faith Joseph, when he was dying, made mention of the exodus of the sons of Israel, and he gave a command[42] concerning his bones.

If we truly have genuine faith; then, we would be very eager to help our family to place their hope in the promises of God. Even though the promises of God was not fulfilled in the lifetime of these patriarchs, their faith was so great; their priority was sharing that hope with each generation, making sure their children cherished their relationship with the Father. Therefore, "Isaac blessed Jacob and Esau concerning things to come." 'In addition, "Jacob, as he was dying, blessed each of the sons of Joseph [Ephraim and Manasseh], and worshiped, leaning on the top of his staff." Joseph had such great faith in the promises of God, especially that his people would inherit the Land of Canaan, he commanded them that they take his bones with them when they departed long after his death. (Genesis 27:27-29, 38-40; 48:8-22; 50:24-26) Are we operating by faith?

Faith Moves Us to Put God First

Hebrews 11:23-26 Updated American Standard Version (UASV)

23 By faith Moses, when he was born, was hidden for three months by his parents, because they saw he was a beautiful child; and they did not fear the edict of the king. 24 By faith Moses, when he had grown up, refused to be called the son of the daughter of Pharaoh, 25 choosing to be ill-treated with the people of God rather than to have the temporary enjoyment of sin, 26 considering the reproach of Christ greater riches than the treasures of Egypt; for he was looking to the reward.

---

42 Or *gave instructions; gave orders*

If we truly have genuine faith; then, we will place God ahead of everything this world has to offer us. The Israelites were made slaves in Egypt after the death of Joseph, in dire need of being delivered, when the parents of Moses took action. "They did not fear the edict of the king," which was to kill every Hebrew male at birth. Rather, when Moses was born, they hid him for three months. "But when she could hide him no longer, she got a papyrus basket for him, and she coated it with tar and with pitch. She put the child in it and placed it among the reeds by the bank of the Nile. And his sister [Miriam] stood at a distance to know what would be done to him. Now the daughter of Pharaoh came down to bathe at the river while her young women walked beside the river. She saw the basket among the reeds and she sent her slave girl, and she took it." (Ex. 2:1-10) The daughter of Pharaoh had a Hebrew woman nurse baby Moses, which actually was his mother, Jochebed. Therefore, Moses was initially nursed and spiritually trained by his father Amram and his mother, Jochebed. Then, growing up under the roof of the Pharaoh's daughter, Moses was instructed in all the wisdom of the Egyptians, and he was mighty in his words and deeds. – Acts 7:20-22.

However, an Egyptian education and the wealth of the Egyptian Empire did not result in Moses abandoning his faith in the only true God. Rather, "when he had grown up, refused to be called the son of the daughter of Pharaoh," a path underscored when he defended a Hebrew brother. (Exodus 2:11-12) Moses chose "to be ill-treated with the people of God [Fellow Israelites] rather than to have the temporary enjoyment of sin." If we are a true servant of God, who has maintained a prayer life, regular meeting attendance, personal Bible study, preparing for Christian meetings, and sharing God's Word, we are following Moses' example, taking a firm stand for pure worship. The battle for true worship is raging even more so today than any other time and, we need to take a stand.

Moses left the house of Pharaoh to join God's chosen people, "considering the reproach of Christ greater riches than the treasures of Egypt; for he was looking to the reward." In other words, Moses valued the reproach of being the ancient type of Christ (Messiah), i.e., anointed one, as greater riches than the treasures of Egypt. John Macarthur writes, "Moses suffered reproach for the sake of Christ in the sense that he identified with Messiah's people in their suffering (v. 25). In addition, Moses identified himself with the Messiah because of his own role as leader and prophet (cf. 12:2; Deut. 18:15; Pss. 69:9; 89:51). Moses knew of the sufferings and glory of the Messiah (cf. John 5:46; Acts 26:22, 23; 1 Pet. 1:10–12). Anyone who suffers because of genuine faith in God and for the redemptive gospel suffers for the sake of Christ (cf. 13:12, 13; 1 Pet. 4:14)."[43] Being a member of Pharaoh's house, Moses could have enjoyed a life of luxury, wealth, power, and prestige. However, by faith, he was "looking to the reward."

Hebrews 11:27-29 Updated American Standard Version (UASV)

[27] By faith he left Egypt, not fearing the wrath of the king; for he endured, as seeing him who is invisible. [28] By faith he kept the Passover, and the sprinkling of the blood, that the destroyer of the firstborn should not touch them. [29] By faith they passed through the Red Sea as on dry land, but when the Egyptians attempted it, they were swallowed up.[44]

Faith can also make us fearless in the face of difficulty, even death, because we have complete trust in God as a deliverer. When Pharaoh heard of it that Moses had killed an Egyptian, he sought to kill Moses. However, Moses fled from Pharaoh and stayed in the land of Midian. (Ex. 2:11-15) In the above, the book of Hebrews is alluding to forty years later, when the Israelites had to exodus Egypt, saying, "By faith he [Moses] left Egypt, not fearing the wrath of the king [who threatened Moses with death for being a representative of God to the Israelites]; for he [Moses] endured, as seeing him who is invisible." (Ex. 10:28-29) Even though Moses had never seen God, His interactions with Moses were so real; it was as though Moses was "seeing him who is invisible." (Ex. 33:20) If we fully commit ourselves to God, fully trusting in him, he will act on our behalf. Can we say that our relationship with God is that strong, or do we waver in difficult times? – Psalm 37:5; Proverbs 16:3.

Just before their exodus from Egypt, "By faith he kept the Passover, and the sprinkling of the blood, that the destroyer of the firstborn should not touch them [i.e., the Israelites]." There is little doubt; it had to of taken faith to keep the Passover, being certain that the firstborn of Israel would come away unscathed while those of the Egyptians would die. Moses faith was rewarded. (Exodus 12:1-39) God proved to be a great deliverer, as the Israelites "passed through the Red Sea as on dry land, but when the Egyptians attempted it, they were swallowed up." The book of Exodus tells us "Israel saw the great hand[45] that Jehovah used against Egypt, and the people feared Jehovah, and they believed in Jehovah and in Moses his servant." (Exodus 14:21-31) The faith of the patriarchs and Moses are a great model for Christians today.

---

[43] MacArthur, John (2005-05-09). *The MacArthur Bible Commentary* (Kindle Locations 62689-62692). Thomas Nelson. Kindle Edition.

[44] Or *they were drowned*

[45] Or *power*

ABEL

(A'bel) [possibly, Exhalation; Vanity]. The second son of Adam and his wife Eve, and the younger brother of their firstborn son, Cain. (Ge 4:2) The absence of the verb *harah* (Gen. 4:2; compare verse Gen. 1:1-31) has been taken to imply, perhaps truly, that Cain and Abel were twins.

Living at the Foundation of the World

Abel began his life at the very beginning of human history. Jesus spoke of this time when he said of Abel, "the foundation of the world." (Lu 11:50-51) Jesus seemed to be speaking of the foundation of humans (humanity) that were redeemable from inherited sin. Abel was the second human to be born and the fourth human on earth, but he was the first who possessed redeemable qualities. While Abel lived close to the time of perfection, those among him were anything but perfect. The world of imperfect humanity was just underway, and it was a time of great sadness for the parents who rejected God and brought on this sin, old age, and death.

Abel often mused, As I woke each day, I saw to very beautiful parents, my mother, and father, Adam and Eve, beautiful people who were positive in attitude and full of energy and new ideas. I struggled at times at the realization, these loving, caring parents had brought about a fallen world, which I could see the awareness of this on their faces from time-to-time. I sometimes wonder what it must have been like to be a perfect human having eternal life before them. I had asked my mother many times and she always seemed to dodge the question with a regretful look on her face. I could not see why my parents rebelled against Jehovah, which resulted in their being banished from the paradise, the Garden of Eden I had never seen. I have known nothing but love from them, how could my mother and father have put their own desires ahead of humanity that was yet to come and their Heavenly Father? My generous parents lost perfection and eternal life for all of us. This might be why Cain was angry all of the time. – Gen 2:15–3:24.

My father had often spoken of life after being exiled from the garden. He told us, boys, many times that their existence now was far harder than when they lived in Eden. My mother has spoken about the pain of giving birth to my bother but that it was also a blessing. Mother remembers her exact words just after the birth, "I have gotten a man with the help of Jehovah." Soon thereafter, mother gave birth to me, naming me Abel. her second son.

Abel Develops His Faith

Cain and I grew up and our father, Adam trained us in the different types of work that was needed to care for our future families. My brother Cain decided to take up farming and I became a shepherd. Over the years of hearing my father talk about God, I began to trust in our Creator that I had never heard or seen. In this, I felt alone because Cain seemed to be so distant and wanted nothing to do with our Creator. Even though I was alone, I could see and feel my love for my Heavenly Father growing day-by-day.

Even though the Creator had cursed the ground, which initially produced thorns and thistles for us, in time, with much hard work, father and us boys had produced enough food to live. The beauty was that God did not curse everything, for there was no curse on the animals, which would include those on dry ground and in the rivers and the sea. I have sat by the rivers many times, staring at the beautiful skies, clouds, sun by day, and the moon and stars by night. When I looked at the grandeur and beauty of what God had created for my parents, my feelings grew as I saw the profound love, wisdom, and goodness of God, the one who created all that my eyes could take in and I could only imagine if Father had net rebelled what things might have been like. (See Romans 1:20) The night was most special to me, I felt strengthened and invigorated by the vastness of the night sky. The nights are countless where I sat there talking aloud to God for hours about the wonderment of life. I know God had spoken to my Father in Eden, but we had not heard his voice since.

I wandered through the land with my flock of gentle sheep daily, walking an unknowable distance each day over hills, through the valleys, and across the trickling streams, always seeking the greenest grass. I am ever watchful for the best places to water my sheep, the well-sheltered places to rest. My love was for the helpless sheep, God's beautiful creatures, always needing my loving guidance, direction, and my protection. I often ponder late into the night if God had designed the sheep to need such human nurturing. This made me come to the realization of just how much I need my loving Heavenly Father, my Creator to guide me through life, for his wisdom and power is far superior to mine. My aloud prayers were filled with such thoughts, which has caused my trust in Him to grow greater day-by-day.

As for me and my brother, Cain, while we were growing into adulthood, mother and father shared the events that took place in the Garden of Eden, which led to God expelling them. What Father tried to inculcate into us is that we should not blame the Creator, for it was Eve who was deceived into giving credence to the words of a serpent, tricked into reaching out for lies, complete falsehoods. And it was father's free will decision to choose Even over his Heavenly Father, an act of rebellion. Father told us again and again that God had forewarned him, and he had warned our mother of what would happen and it was they, father and mother, who chose not to listen. Many nights I meditated on these words from my parents.

When father explained the curses that were to take place because of their rebellion, I could clearly see the thorns and thistles that fulfilled those words of God. While I was not there for the childbirth of my brother Cain, mother spoke of the pains of pregnancy and labor pains before delivering my brother. Mother had also seemed to seek father's love and attention excessively, which was in line with the Words of God as well. What I learned from these and other things is this, when the Creator says anything, it is absolutely trustworthy. I have complete trust in him.

When I was but a boy, I would sneak out to see the materialized cherubim. They left me feeling deep emotions as you could tell that they wielded great power. I was in great wonder at the ever-flaming, whirling sword. It never mattered what time of the day I came to watch the cherubim, they never moved, the sword never stopped. I mean there are times when I get bored with my shepherding and sneak away for some adventures but never the cherubim. These powerful creatures were ever loyal day after day, month after month, year after year, and decade after decade, never moving from that spot. These were forever steadfastly faithful to what God had assigned them to do, unlike my mother and Father, and now Cain as well. These mighty creatures caused my faith in God to be strengthened.

One day, like many others, I walked with my sheep through the pasture within a valley, surrounded by the most beautiful tree. To my right, I could still see the soft glow in the distance. I knew between those ridges at the east side of the garden God had put living creatures [the cherubim] and a flaming sword which turned in all directions. "This was to keep anyone from coming near the tree that gives life." I knew that my Father, Adam, and my mother Eve, had once lived there. However, it has been many years since before Cain, my elder brother's birth that my parents could enter. It was late evening and the wind was blowing through the valley, as I walked with my sheep, I could feel the cool breeze on my face. I do not know whether it is the cool wind that brought a chill to my bones or my thoughts of the Creator, whom I knew so very well because my Father had spoken of him often. I stopped abruptly and was moved to words similar to ones that I had often uttered. "Jehovah God," I cried aloud from deep within my chest, my heart beating ever faster, "will the transgression between my parents and you ever be healed?" I went on, "This is the one desire in my young life that alluded me, Father."

A Shepherd

"Abel was a keeper of sheep, but Cain was a tiller of the ground," thus representing the two fundamental pursuits of civilized life, the two earliest subdivisions of the human race. The narrative may possibly bear witness to the primitive idea that pastoral life was more pleasing to Jehovah than the care, cultivation, and breeding of crops and animals.

Cain and Abel, having been instructed, perhaps by their father, Adam, in the duty of worship to their Creator, each offered the first-fruits of his labors: Cain, as a man who cultivated the land; a farmer, the fruits of the field; Abel, as a shepherd, fatlings of his flock. God was pleased to accept the offering of Abel, in preference to that of his brother (**Heb 11:4**), in consequence of which Cain, giving himself up to envy, formed the desire of killing Abel; which he at length effected, having invited him to go into the field (**Ge 4:8-9**; comp. **1 John 3:12**). The Jews had a tradition that Abel was murdered in the plain of Damascus; and accordingly, his tomb is still shown on a high hill near the village of Sinie or Seneiah, about twelve miles northwest of Damascus, on the road to Baalbek (Jerome, in Ezechiel 37). The summit of the hill is still called *Nebi Abel;* but circumstances lead to the probable supposition that this was the site, or in the vicinity of the site, of the ancient Abela or Abila. The legend, therefore, was most likely suggested by the ancient name of the place.

A True Worshipper

"In process of time," the two brothers came in a solemn manner to sacrifice unto Jehovah, in order to express their gratitude to Him whose tenants they were in the land (Gen. 4:3-4). How Jehovah signified His acceptance of the one offering and rejection of the other, we are not told. That it was due to the difference in the material of the sacrifice or in their manner of offering was probably the belief among the early Israelites, who regarded animal offerings as superior to cereal offerings. Both kinds, however, were fully in accord with Hebrew law and custom. It has been suggested that the Septuagint rendering of Gen. 4:7 makes Cain's offense a ritual one, the offering not being "correctly" made or rightly divided, and hence rejected as irregular. "Have you not sinned if you offer rightly but do not divide rightly? Be still!" (LEB) The Septuagint evidently took the rebuke to turn upon Cain's neglect to prepare his offering according to strict ceremonial requirements. The Septuagint of Genesis 4:7 (Gr. *dieles*) suggests that the offense of Cain was a ritual one, in that, the offering was not presented properly. However, strict ceremonial regulations only applied to animal sacrifices. Compare Ex. 29:17; Lev. 8:20; Judges 19:29; 1 Ki 18:23.

A Righteous Man

The true reason for the Divine preference is doubtless to be found in the disposition of the brothers. Well-doing consisted not in the outward offering (Ge 4:7) but in the right state of mind and feeling. The acceptability depends on the inner motives and moral characters of the offerers. "By faith Abel offered to God a better sacrifice (more abundant more acceptable, of greater value or importance, *pleiona*) than Cain." (Heb 11:4) The more abundant more acceptable, of greater value or importance, (*pleiona*) than Cains, says, "The phrase 'than Cain did' can be connected with Abel or with his 'sacrifice' in the sense of a sacrifice that is better than Cain's." Who was Abel's sacrifice accepted and Cain's rejected? Cain's heart was no longer pure; it had a criminal propensity, springing from envy and jealousy, which rendered both his offering and person unacceptable. His evil works and hatred of his brother culminated in the act of murder, specifically evoked by the opposite character of Abel's works and the acceptance of his offering. The evil man cannot endure the sight of goodness in another.

A Martyr

Abel ranks as the first martyr (Matt. 23:35), whose blood cried for vengeance (Gen. 4:10; compare Re 6:9-10) and brought despair (Gen. 4:13), whereas that of Jesus appeals to God for forgiveness and speaks peace (Heb. 12:24) and is preferred before Abel's.

A Type

The first two brothers in history stand as the types and representatives of the two main and enduring divisions of mankind, and bear witness to the absolute antithesis and eternal enmity between good and evil.

The Superiority of His Offering

Over the years, I knew my faith was growing until I could stand it no more, I had to evidence it with some kind of action. As I moved amongst the sheep in my flock, I pondered to myself, as I had done many times. It all seemed so futile for so long. "What do I have that I could ever offer the one who created my father and my mother. What can the created, me, a mere human, give to the almighty, the all-powerful Creator of all things?" One night by the fire, I was looking up at the stars, a heartfelt truth came to me as I lowered his eyes from the heavens to my sheep in the field. How had this escaped me for so many years? "All I have to do is have the right motive as I offer Jehovah God the best of my flock, and I know my heavenly Father will be pleased with me." At that moment, I felt a peace come over me that I had never felt before. I struggled to sleep through the night, as I was anxious to get back home and share the news with my parents and my older brother, Cain.

The next day, it seemed like it took me forever to make my way home with the flock moving slower than they ever had before, or was it just my anxiousness at the idea of sharing this revelation of mine? Finally, as I neared the home, I began running the rest of the way. I came upon my brother first and explained how this profound truth came to me the night before. Cain glared at me with his usual disdain, raising his voice in exasperation, "You are always looking to find favor in everyone's eyes. from mother to Father, and now the Creator?" Cain pushed me to the ground, mockingly saying, "What will this God whom you have never seen or ever heard from want from a lowly human such as yourself?" Pulling myself up from the ground, I shook off my brother's normal negative spirit and abusive words, as I rushed off to share his thoughts with mother and father. After telling them of the experience of the night before, they responded in the way that I had wished Cain would have, with love and support. So, the next day, I prepared to offer up some of the very best sheep from my flock. I could see that Cain was watching me from a distance, seething once more over my desire to seek out ways to please those whom I deeply love.

Cain was angry with Abel and he was not going to look bad in father's eyes once more, so he too went about preparing his offering from his crops. Yet, Cain was only half-listening to his younger brother the day before, so the whole 'right motive' was lost on him. However, it would become apparent the moment the offerings were being presented. Abel, again, took notice of what he thought was Cain preparing to seek God's blessings and favor too. His heart was warmed at the idea his brother had heard his words. However, he did not realize that his words had fallen on deaf ears, for his brother was only making a showy display for his parents, not even really considering the Creator. Abel always thought the best of his older brother even through all of the verbal and physical abuse.

I built an altar and used fire for my offering. My brother in his efforts to find favor in Father's eyes built an even more impressive looking altar for his sacrifice by fire. We had built our altars at the edge of the valley where I received my revelation. It was within sight of the cherubs and the glowing sword. I wanted this to be in the presence of the only living representatives of our Heavenly Father here on earth. I and my brother Cain heard a voice from heaven say, "I have found favor with you Abel and your offering." (Gen. 4:4) At that moment, I fell to my knees, and said, "Father I have offered you myself and the best from my flock."

I must admit that I was a bit perplexed, 'was it my offering itself that pleased God?' I did offer him the best living, breathing creature, shedding its precious lifeblood. I do know that my revelation was of me having the right motive as I offered Jehovah God the very best of my flock, and I knew that my heavenly Father would be pleased and find favor with me as well as my offering because my motivations were pure. My heart was motivated by love and by genuine faith, which is why I was moved to make the offering. Nevertheless, God's voice from heaven was still a shock to me.

Abel was unaware that centuries after he was murdered, Jehovah had humans offer an unblemished lamb to picture the sacrifice of God's own perfect Son, "the Lamb of God, who takes away the sin of the world." (John 1:29; Exodus 12:5-7) Yet, the revelation of Abel was simply a general sense of what was needed, with no clear picture of what was going to be needed, all of that was beyond Abel's knowledge or understanding at that time of his martyrdom.

I was looking on now as my brother Cain made his offering. As Cain went about presenting some of the land's produce as an offering, God's voice came from heaven once more, "Cain, I have found no favor in you and upon your offering." I was stunned and a bit worried knowing my brother. I could see from here that he was furious, and he looked dejected. The rage in his eyes was apparent for all to see and it shook me to the core.

Cain's offering was not rejected because of what he offered; it was more. Later, under the Mosaic Law, God allowed the offering of the produce of the land. (Lev. 6:14-15) It would be some 4,000 years later that the Apostle John would say that Cain "was of the evil one." (1 John 3:12) It was not what Cain did but how he had done it, it was a mere outward devotion to God that was focused on mimicking his brother so as to not look bad before his Father, Adam. He had no real or genuine faith or love for the Creator. In fact, he despised the Creator because of being the inherited human imperfection that was to lead to his death.

When Cain had seen that once again, it was Abel who had found favor in his parent's eyes and especially when he heard the words from the Creator, favoring Abel, he did not seek out his father, Adam, to find out why. No, he stewed on this, seething with rage, hating his brother more than he ever had. What Cain did not realize was the God was still watching and could read his heart, the seat of motivation. Our loving heavenly Father knew what Cain's reaction would be before he ever offered to reason with him. Yet, he reasoned with Cain anyway. Jehovah's voice came from heaven once more, saying to Cain, "Why are you furious? And why do you look despondent? If you do what is right, won't you be accepted? But if you do not do what is right, sin is crouching at the door. Its desire is for you, but you must rule over it." (Gen 4:6-7) Cain's heart was beyond reason, hardened beyond repentance.

I was standing near my altar when I saw Cain walking toward me. His face was blank, no real expression of anything. He stopped before me. Cain said to me, "Abel, 'Let's go out to the field.'" I was a bit nervous but responded, "sure Cain, sure." As we walked toward the field, I tried to let him know that everything will be okay. "Cain do not worry, the Creator is a loving God and if we turn toward him and worship him with our whole heart, he is a forgiving God. As we entered into the field, I was still talking on about how everything will be fine when I felt this sharp pain in the back of my head. I fell to my knees, reaching back and pulling my hand forward, to find it covered in blood. In the first real pain I ever knew, I look up at Cain to find him swinging this club toward my face and then it all went black.

Cain had ignored God's warning. He had said to his brother Abel, "Let's go out to the field." And while they were in the field, Cain attacked his brother Abel and killed him. Then Jehovah said to Cain, "Where is your brother Abel?" "I don't know," he replied. "Am I my brother's guardian?" – Genesis 4:8-9. At that moment, Abel became the first victim of religious persecution, the very first martyr. Although he died, his life lesson still lives on in the pages of God's Word.

Then God said to Cain "What have you done? **Your brother's blood cries out to me** from the ground! So now you are cursed, alienated from the ground that opened its mouth to receive your brother's blood you have shed. If you work the ground, it will never again give you its yield. You will be a restless wanderer on the earth." (Genesis 4:10-12) Yes, in a figurative sense Abel's blood is still crying out to us today. The great faith of Abel is what speaks out to us today. He lived a little more than one hundred years in a time when persons lived almost one thousand years. Nevertheless, the years he had was spent better than any of the preflood people. The last breath he drew was in knowing that minutes earlier God had said, "I have found favor with you Abel and your offering." (Gen 4:4) The apostle Paul would write almost 4,000 years later, "By faith Abel offered to God a better sacrifice than Cain did. By faith he was approved as a righteous man, because God approved his gifts, and even though he is dead, he still speaks through his faith." (Heb. 11:4) We can be certain that Abel will receive a resurrection. (John 5:28-29) There is even the chance of our meeting Abel one day even though he is dead, if he still speaks to us through his faith.

Bible Difficulties Answered Surrounding Adam and Eve and Cain and Abel

Defining Bible Difficulties

Bible critics be they atheists, agnostics, Muslims, and so on, want to tell us that there are mistakes, errors, and contradictions in the Bible. In fact, they would like us to believe that the Bible is filled with such things. They make this claim because they view the 40+ Bible authors as mere 'men writing the Bible' However, we can reply, 'It is true. About 40+ imperfect men wrote the Bible. But what you call mistakes, errors, or contradictions are actually Bible difficulties. What are Bible difficulties? They are difficulties that arise because the Old Testament 39 Bible books were written 3,500 years ago to 2,500 years ago in ancient Hebrew and Aramaic languages, within dozens of different ancient cultures. The New Testament 27 Bible books were written 2,000 years ago over a fifty-year period in the Koine Greek language, within many different ancient cultures. Thus, difficulties arise because we are from modern-day culture thousands of years removed translating and interpreting ancient languages.

Below are a number of Bible difficulties that go with our historical fiction account of Adam and Eve and Cain and Abel.

Genesis 1:27 BDC: Were Adam and Eve Allegorical or Historical Persons?

Critical Scholars either consider Adam and Eve as a myth or symbolic persons, representing humankind. The evidence from the Bible, on the other hand, is that they are real historical persons. Before looking at the biblical evidence, let us note that Hebrew manuscripts are archaeological evidence that gives us the historicity of humanity. The oldest manuscripts date to the 3rd century B.C.E. In addition, Greek New Testament manuscripts give us how Jewish Christians from the first century, as well as the Son of God, views the Hebrew Old Testament and the historicity of Adam and Eve, and these NT MSS are archaeological evidence, some even dating as early as the second-century C.E.[46]

Scriptural Evidence

(1) Genesis 1-2 is a historical narrative that expounds on Adam and Eve's creation and events within their lives. (2) They are recorded as giving birth to children, as do the others mentioned in the early genealogies. (Gen 4:1, 25; 5:1) (3) The Hebrew word toledoth, often translated "generations," should be translated "history" at Genesis 2:4; 5:1; 6:9; 10:1; 11:10; as well as five other places in Genesis. Regardless, it shows that toledoth is used all throughout Genesis, in speaking of descendants of so-and-so, and has the same meaning in its use with Adam and Eve at Genesis 5:1. (4) If we look at the chronologies throughout the Old Testament, Adam starts the list. (1 Ch 1:1) (5) All early humankind did not father Seth. No, Adam fathered him at the specific age of 130 years. (Gen 5:3) (6) Luke places Adam at the start of human history. (Lu 3:38) (7) Jesus viewed Adam and Eve as real historical persons. (Matt 19:24-25) (8) The inheritance of sin and death came from a literal Adam. (Rom 5:12-14) (9) Jesus is contrasted with Adam, which means if we deny Adam as a historical person, we deny Jesus Christ and his sacrifice as well. (1 Cor. 15:45-47) (10) Again, Paul comes to the stage as a witness, when he informs us that Adam was created first and then Eve. (1 Tim 2:13-14) (11) Was Enoch the seventh in line from all early humankind? (Jude14) Reasonably, humankind had to of started from just two people at some time. The fact is that the Bible, as a reliable book and archaeological evidence of human history, gives us those two individuals, Adam and Eve.

Has Science Now Caught Up With the Fact That All of Us Descended from the Same Original Parents?

Dr. Purdom explains:

---

[46] **Common Era:** B.C.E. means "before the Common Era," which is more accurate than B.C. ("before Christ"). C.E. denotes "Common Era," often called A.D., for *anno Domini,* meaning "in the year of our Lord."

The genetic evidence is consistent with human DNA being "young" and the human race beginning with a very small starting population (the Bible tells us the starting population was two people!).

The International HapMap project endeavors to study a select group of DNA similarities and differences between humans known as single nucleotide polymorphisms (SNPs).[47] The SNPs are believed to be representative of the genome (total human DNA) such that what is true for them would be true for the whole genome. These studies and others have shown that the difference in DNA between any two humans is amazingly low . . . only 0.1 percent.[48]

Reflecting on this very low percentage, some scientists posited, "This proportion is low compared with those of many other species, from fruit flies to chimpanzees, reflecting the recent origins of our species from a small founding population" (emphases mine).[49] They also stated, "[Certain genetic estimates] tell us that humans vary only slightly at the DNA level and that only a small proportion of this variation separates continental populations."[50]

These findings are consistent with the Bible's history that humans were created several thousand years ago; in other words, a short amount of time has passed, so there is little genetic variation.

The Bible Concurs

Acts 17:26 Updated American Standard Version (UASV)

and he [God] made from one man every nation of mankind to live on all the face of the earth, having determined their appointed times and the boundaries of their habitation,

How does the Bible View Adam?

Jude 14 Updated American Standard Version (UASV)

[47] HapMap Homepage
[48] Lynn B. Jorde and Stephen P. Wooding, "Genetic Variation, Classification and 'Race'," Nature Genetics 36 (2004): S28–S33. Quoted in "Were Adam and Eve Real People," chapter 20 of How We Know the Bible is True volume 2, Green Forest, Arkansas: Master Books, 2012.
[49] IBID
[50] IBID

EDWARD D. ANDREWS

¹⁴ It was also about these men that Enoch, the seventh one in line from Adam,[51] prophesied, saying, "Behold, the Lord came with tens of thousands of his holy ones,

Note here that Jude makes a historical reference to Enoch being the seventh in line from Adam, not all, early mankind.

Luke 3:23-38 Updated American Standard Version (UASV)

²³ Jesus, when he began his ministry, was about thirty years of age, being the son (as was supposed) of Joseph, the son of Heli, . . . ³¹ son of David . . . ³⁴ son of Abraham . . . ³⁷ son of Adam."

Both David and Abraham are well-known historical persons, so why would Luke go through the genealogy of all many historical persons to get back to an allegorical person? Would not the Jews know if Adam were an allegorical person? Would it not make a genealogical list look quite silly if one took it back to an allegorical person?

Genesis 5:3 Updated American Standard Version (UASV)

³ When Adam had lived one hundred and thirty years, he became[52] the father of a son in his own likeness, according to his image, and named him Seth.

So, if Adam is allegorical, standing for early mankind, how do we reason that early mankind fathered Seth, specifically at 130 years of age?

Can the fact that we have a serpent speaking to Eve be used to argue for an allegorical story?

Genesis 3:1-4 Updated American Standard Version (UASV)

3 Now the serpent was more crafty than any beast of the field which Jehovah God had made. And he said to the woman, "Did God actually say, 'You[53] shall not eat of any tree in the garden'?" ² And the woman said to the serpent, "From the fruit of the trees of the garden we may eat, ³ but from the tree that is in the midst of the garden, God said, 'You shall not eat from it, nor shall you touch it, lest you die.'" ⁴ And the **serpent said to the woman,** "You shall not surely die.

John 8:44 Updated American Standard Version (UASV)

⁴⁴ You are of your father the devil, and your will is to do your father's desires. That one was a manslayer from the beginning, and does not stand

---

[51] Following the genealogy of Genesis 5:1–24; 1 Chronicles 1:1–3, Enoch was the seventh in the line of Adam. – MacArthur, John (2005-05-09). *The MacArthur Bible Commentary* (Kindle Locations 66202-66203). Thomas Nelson. Kindle Edition.
[52] Lit begot
[53] In Hebrew *you* is plural in verses 1–5

in the truth, because there is no truth in him. When he lies, he speaks out of his own character, for he is a liar and the father of lies.

We see here that Jesus, whose historicity is settled states unambiguously that Satan the Devil was the one behind the first lie in the Garden of Eden. Satan, a powerful angel (specifically a Cherub), spoke through the serpent, just as a ventriloquist can make his voice come through a dummy.

Revelation 12:9 Updated American Standard Version (UASV)

[9] And the great dragon was thrown down, the serpent of old who is called the devil and Satan, who deceives the whole inhabited earth; he was thrown down to the earth, and his angels were thrown down with him.

If we say the first man Adam was allegorical, what does that mean for Jesus Christ, as we know he is not allegorical, making the contrast in Corinthians meaningless.

1 Corinthians 15:45, 47 Updated American Standard Version (UASV)

[45] So also it is written, "The first man, Adam, became a living soul." The last Adam became a life-giving spirit ... [47] The first man is from the earth and made of dust; the second man is from heaven.

If we deny the historicity of Adam and his sin, a rebellion against God, it would mean the denial of the purpose of Jesus Christ's coming. Such a rejection is a motive for the anti-miracle Bible critics, activist atheists, who want such a rejection to be a repudiation of the Christian faith.

How did Jesus himself view the Genesis?

Matthew 19:4-5 Updated American Standard Version (UASV)

[4] And he answered and said, "Have you not read that he who created them from the beginning made them male and female, [5] and said, 'For this reason a man shall leave his father and mother and be joined to his wife, and the two shall become one flesh'?

Clearly, Jesus viewed the Genesis account to be factual and historical. If we look at the entire sixty-six books of the Bible, which covered 1,600 years of the history of the Israelite nation, written by forty+ men, all of which a belief in a historical Adam, it would seem that while we do not have archaeological evidence for the historicity of Adam, we have archaeological evidence that references him as being a historical person that goes back to the third century B.C.E. up unto the sixteenth century C.E., i.e., well over 33,000 manuscripts. The irony is, those same secularists would not reject a real historical person, with far less evidence.

Sumeria

The first recorded name given in an actual writing system can be found on clay tablets dating from the Jemdet Nasr period in Sumeria between 3200 and 3101 BC.[54]

Example of Jemdet Nasr cuneiform (Credit: Metropolitan Museum of Art

The tablets are not profound treatises on human thinking, but accounting ledgers for tallying up goods and possessions! Some of the first names are those of the slave owner Gal-Sal and his two slaves Enpap-x and Sukkalgir (3200-3100 BC). Another name is that of Turgunu Sanga (3100 BC) who seems to have been an accountant for the Turgunu family. There are many more names from this period but none that appear much before 3200 BC.[55]

What Is Recorded History?

Recorded history or written history is a historical narrative based on a written record or other documented communication. Recorded history can be contrasted with other narratives of the past such as mythological or oral traditions.

---

[54] Who Was the First Named Human? - The Huffington Post, http://www.huffingtonpost.com/dr-sten-odenwald/who-was-the-first-named-h_b_56798 (accessed March 24, 2020).

[55] Who Was the First Named Human? - The Huffington Post, http://www.huffingtonpost.com/dr-sten-odenwald/who-was-the-first-named-h_b_56798 (accessed March 24, 2020).

Historical Method

The historical method comprises the techniques and guidelines by which historians use primary sources and other evidence to research and then to write history. Primary sources are firsthand evidence of history (usually written, but sometimes captured in other mediums) made at the time of an event by a present person. Historians think of those sources as the closest to the origin of the information or idea under study.[56] These types of sources can provide researchers with, as Dalton and Charnigo put it, "direct, unmediated information about the object of study."[57]

Historians use other types of sources to understand history as well. Secondary sources are written accounts of history based upon the evidence from primary sources. These are sources which, usually, are accounts, works, or research that analyze, assimilate, evaluate, interpret, and/or synthesize primary sources. Tertiary sources are compilations based upon primary and secondary sources and often tell a more generalized account built on the more specific research found in the first two types of sources.[58]

It should be mentioned again that the Hebrew manuscripts that date to the 3rd, 2nd and 1st centuries B.C.E. are copies of what came down from the originals, which date to as early as middle of the 16th century B.C.E. Moreover, the Dead Sea community believed and wrote that Adam was a real historical person, based on their earliest manuscripts.

Manuscript 4QMMT (also known as the Halakhic Letter or the Sectarian Manifesto, later called Some Precepts of the Law) states, "We have written to you so that you should understand the Book of Moses and the Books of the Prophets and David."

This is one of if not the earliest reference to the custom of subdividing the Scriptures into three parts—'the law of Moses, the Prophets, and the Psalms.' It supports Jesus words, "These are My words which I spoke to you while I was still with you, that all things which are written about Me in the Law of Moses and the Prophets and the Psalms must be fulfilled." (Lu 24:44) The Jewish historian Josephus is in harmony with this text as well

---

[56] User Education Services. "Primary, Secondary and Tertiary Sources". University of Maryland Libraries. Retrieved March 24, 2020. "Library Guides: Primary, secondary and tertiary sources"

[57] Dalton, Margaret Steig; Charnigo, Laurie (2004). "Historians and Their Information Sources" (PDF). College & Research Libraries. September: 400–25, at 416 n.3, citing U.S. Dept. of Labor, Bureau of Labor Statistics (2003), Occupational Outlook Handbook; Lorenz, C. (2001). "History: Theories and Methods". In Smelser, Neil J.; Bates. International Encyclopedia of Social and Behavior Sciences

[58] User Education Services. "Primary, Secondary and Tertiary Sources". University of Maryland Libraries. Retrieved March 24, 2020. Amsterdam: Elsevier. p. 6871 "Library Guides: Primary, secondary and tertiary sources"

(I, 38-40 [8]) around the year 100 C.E., as he confirms the close of the Hebrew Scriptures cannon at the time of Malachi. He wrote, "We do not possess myriads of inconsistent books, conflicting with each other. Our books, those which are justly accredited, are but two and twenty [counted as thirty-nine today] and contain the record of all time. Of these, five are the books of Moses, comprising the laws and the traditional history from the birth of man down to the death of the lawgiver. . . . From the death of Moses until Artaxerxes [i.e., 475-424 B.C.E., who succeeded Xerxes as king of Persia, the prophets subsequent to Moses wrote the history of the events of their own times in thirteen books. The remaining four books contain hymns to God and precepts for the conduct of human life."

Genesis 2:17 BDC: Why did Adam and Eve not die in the day that they ate of the fruit from the forbidden tree?

God at Genesis 2:17 warned Adam of "the tree of the knowledge of good and evil you shall not eat, for in the day that you eat of it you shall surely die." It would seem that when Adam passed that warning on to Eve, she took it very seriously because she expanded on and emphasized the warning when speaking with the serpent. The woman said to the serpent, God said, 'You shall not eat of the fruit of the tree that is in the midst of the garden, neither shall you touch it, lest you die.'" (Gen 3:3) You will notice that she added, "neither shall you touch it." "But the serpent said to the woman, "'You will not surely die.'" (Gen 3:4) Was the serpent (i.e., Satan), telling the truth, as Adam would go on to live for another 930-years? (Gen. 5:5) No, Satan lied! In the day of their eating the fruit of the forbidden tree, they died spiritually.

If we look at the context of Adam when he received the command at Genesis 2:17, how would have Adam understood the expression, "in the day that you eat of it"? It is true, that Moses said to God, "For a thousand years in your sight are but as yesterday." (Ps 90:4) In addition, while addressing the extent of Jehovah God's patience, the apostle Peter said, "that with the Lord one day is as a thousand years and a thousand years as one day." (2 Pet 3:8) However, Adam lived and died long before both of these statements and would have had no knowledge of such. It was not as though Adam was thinking of his great love for Eve, and saying to himself, "If I eat of the forbidden tree, I will have one of Jehovah's days to live, a thousand years to spend with Eve. Yes, Adam would have no knowledge with which to reason in such a way. In other words, he would have understood the word "day" to be a literal twenty-four-hour day. God does not speak ambiguously, and he would have expressed himself in order to be understood, according to what Adam would know as to the terms that were used. Thus, God meant exactly what Adam would have understood it to mean, a twenty-four-hour day. God did not mean, "the tree of the knowledge of good and evil you shall not eat, for in the [thousand-year-long day] that you eat of it you shall surely die." Such a statement as that would have had no force in the mind of Adam; it would have lost all intended force of Jehovah's warning.

Adam would have received the Genesis 2:17 warning directly from God, even if a representative, his only-begotten Son, "the Word", delivered that warning.[iii] This, of course, begs the question, why then did Adam and Eve not die 'in a twenty-four-hour day?' Well, we must ask another question first. As to the Bible, what is death? The *World Book Encyclopedia* (1987, Vol. 5, p. 52b) pointed out: "A person whose heart and lungs stop working may be considered clinically dead, but somatic death may not yet have occurred. The individual cells of the body continue to live for several minutes. The person may be revived if the heart and lungs start working again and give the cells the oxygen they need. After about three minutes, the brain cells, which are most sensitive to a lack of oxygen, begin to die. The person is soon dead beyond any possibility of revival. Gradually, other cells of the body also die. The last ones to perish are the bone, hair, and skin cells, which may continue to grow for several hours." We know that the breathing and the active life force (Heb., *ruach chaiyim*) maintained in the cells by the blood are very important. From this, we can see that it is not the termination of breathing and the heartbeat alone, but also includes the loss of the life force from the body's cells that brings the sort of physical death as spoken of in the Scriptures. Ps 104:29; 146:4; Eccl 8:8.

However, the Scriptures speak of another kind of death, a spiritual death, which is illustrated by the death spoken of above as the condition of humankind at present but is also relative to our discussion as well. In other words, Adam died spiritually on the very day of eating from the forbidden tree, and this would result in old age and eventually death. A man was begging off from following Jesus, saying, "Lord, let me first go and bury my father." Jesus responded, "Leave the dead to bury their own dead. . ." (Lu 9:59-60) The man's father was not dead yet, the son simply wanted to hold off following Jesus until his father died, and was simply looking for a way out. However, Jesus' response, "Leave the dead to bury their own dead," illustrated that spiritually dead and being dead are, in essence, one and the same unless there is some sort of intervention (more on that later) because physical death is the eventuality of those that are spiritually dead.

In addition, we have the apostle Paul referring to the woman living for sensual indulgence as "dead even while she lives." (Lu 9:60; 1Ti 5:6; Eph 2:1) Physical death was the sentence handed down to Adam and thus his descendants as well. However, this was brought about by way of the spiritual death, which affected Adam and Eve the very moment they ate from the forbidden tree. They were now alienated from God, and removed from the symbolic tree of life, being sent out from the Garden of Eden. This alienation is self-evident as the two vainly tried to hide from God, their guilt ridden conscious affecting them. (Gen 3:8) The apostle Paul expressed it as being "dead in the trespasses and sins," becoming "children of wrath." (Eph. 2:1–3)

Romans 6:7 says, "one who has died has been set free from sin." However, Roman 6:2, 11 informs us that a Christian can 'consider themselves dead to sin and alive to God in Christ Jesus." Romans 7:2-6 helps us to appreciate that Christians "are released from the law, having died to that which held us captive, so that we serve in the new way of the Spirit and not in the old way of the written code. Jesus said that he came to earth "to give his life as a ransom for many." (Matthew 20:28).

Adam and Eve were guilty before God and then stood before him in an unrighteous condition. Within this unrighteous condition came a defilement and pollution of a new state of being, fallen flesh (Gr., sarx), which placed Adam and his descendants in an alienated position toward God and in enmity toward him (Rom 8:5-8) Hence, the mindset of imperfect man is mentally bent and geared toward evil. Because of Adam, we are born into sin (missing the mark of perfection) and are looking at the sentence of death. (Ps 51:5; Rom 5:12; Eph 2:3). This was the condition of Adam and Eve, the very moment they willfully chose to rebel against God, and commit that awful transgression. Instantly, they were thrown into the condition of a spiritual death. At that moment there was no hope for the human race, regardless of what any would do in life, the sentence would be death. However, Jehovah is a God of mercy, and while the human race merited death, we received undeserved kindness, which can be found in Genesis 3:15.

As has been stated and is obvious from Scripture, the physical death did not come immediately. God had created them perfectly after all; therefore, they would take far longer to grow older and die. Regardless, they were no longer going to be perfect but had taken on imperfection. God had removed his blessing of them as being good, and, eventually, their imperfection would show signs of growing old and impending death

The penalty was unavoidable. As to justice, from the viewpoint of God, Adam and Eve died that day. (Compare Luke 20:37-38.) However, to fulfill his own will and purpose regarding the inhabiting of the earth, Jehovah permitted them to produce a family before they were to grow old, get sick and die. All the same, while Adam and Eve may not have been aware of God's viewpoint of time, they both did die within one of his days, a thousand years. While there may be no absolute connection between Moses or Peter's statement about the way God views time, it seems a bit too much, to be a mere coincidence that Adam lived to be 930-years, and Methuselah lived to be 969-years, with not one preflood person living beyond a thousand years old.—Genesis 5:3-5; Psalm 90:4; 2 Peter 3:8.

GENESIS 3:5 OTBDC: Is man made in the image of God or does he become like God?

Genesis 3:5 Updated American Standard Version (UASV)

⁵ For God knows that when you eat of it your eyes will be opened, and you will be like God, knowing good and evil." knowing good and evil.

We are told at Genesis 1:27 that "God created man in his own image." However, Genesis 3:22 tells us "the man has become like one of us." It seems that Genesis 1:27 is saying that humans *were made* like God, while Genesis 3:22 is saying that humans *became* like God.

The answer lies in the fact that we are dealing with two different subject matters, and to look at the two together isolated from their individual sections is to take them out of context. Genesis 1 is dealing with the creation of humanity, and that we were *made in* the image of God, something we were given. Genesis 3 is dealing with man's fall into sin, and his willful rebellion against God, rejecting God's sovereignty, God's standard of right and wrong. In this, Adam and Eve had acquired the right to *become* like God in determining for themselves what is right and what is wrong. Genesis 1 is prior to the fall, refers to the nature of Adam and Eve, while Genesis 3 is after the fall, and refers to their state of being.

GENESIS 3:5 OTBDC: What Was the Original Sin of Adam and Eve?

Genesis 3:5-6 Updated American Standard Version (UASV)

5 For God knows that when you eat of it your eyes will be opened, and you will be like God, knowing [Heb. *yada*] good and evil." knowing [Heb. *yada*] good and evil. 6 So when the woman saw that the tree was good for food, and that it was a delight to the eyes, and that the tree was to be desirable to make one wise, and she took of its fruit and ate, then she also gave some to her husband when with her, and he ate.

Was the original sin of Adam and Eve "sexual relations," "knowledge," "disobedience," or "rebellion" against God's sovereignty? Many people for millenniums have thought that the forbidden fruit in the Garden of Eden was actually a symbol of sexual relations. Therefore, the sin was Adam and Eve having sexual relations.

According to the historian Elaine Pagels, "Clement rejects, above all, **the claim that Adam and Eve's sin was to engage in sexual intercourse—**a view common among such Christian teachers as Tatian the Syrian [second-century], who taught that the fruit of the tree of knowledge conveyed *carnal* knowledge. Tatian had pointed out that after Adam and Eve ate the forbidden fruit, they became sexually aware: 'Then the eyes of both were opened, and they knew that they were naked (Genesis 3:7)'"[59] For Augustine of the fifth century C.E., sin had its beginnings in sexual desires. The New Yorker writes, "In the case of 'Your eyes will be opened,' he was certain that there must have been, after all, something that the couple actually saw for the first time after their transgression, something not merely metaphorical: 'They turned their eyes on their own genitals, and lusted after them with that stirring movement they had not previously known.'"[60]

Still, others have claimed that "the tree of the knowledge (Heb. *yada*) of good and evil" represented knowledge itself. Here "knowledge of good and evil" is representative of all knowledge. If this was the case, this would mean that the God of the Bible, who through special revelation exhorted all of his people from the outset to read and study meant for Adam and Eve to remain ignorant. Therefore, their rebellion was them simply trying to increase their knowledge.

---

[59] Elaine Pagels, *Adam, Eve, and the Serpent: Sex and Politics in Early Christianity* (New York, NY: Vintage Books, 1989), 27.
[60] *This article appears in the print edition of the June 19, 2017, issue, with the headline "The Invention of Sex." Stephen Greenblatt is the John Cogan University Professor of the Humanities at Harvard.*

Both of these interpretations do not paint a picture of the God of the Bible but rather some fickle, erratic, moody Creator. Why would a loving God create both Adam and Eve with sexual and intellectual needs and then work against their fulfilling those very desires he gave them, even to the point of threatening them with death? It would be very difficult to love a God such as this.

Was Sex the Original Sin?

Most who would offer such an interpretation are not aware that both the above interpretations contradict the biblical account itself. We will begin with the belief that God's prohibition in the Garden of Eden was actually him forbidding sexual relations. Genesis 2:16-17 reads, "And Jehovah God commanded the man, saying, "From every tree of the garden you may freely eat, but from the tree of the knowledge of good and evil you shall not eat, for in the day that you eat from it you shall surely die."

Yet, when we consider the Creator's command to "be fruitful and multiply and fill the earth" (Gen. 1:28), sexual relations have to be discarded as to what the tree, the fruit, or even what the language represented, for how else would Adam and Eve be able to be obedient to the command to procreate to the point of filling the earth. It would have been impossible for Adam and Eve to be obedient to that command without having sexual relations. Does it really seem reasonable and rational that God would command Adam and Eve to do something and then sentence the to death for being obedient to his command? This view would contradict God's clear command.

In addition, God had commanded Adam not to eat the fruit of "the tree of the knowledge of good and evil" before Eve was even created. (Genesis 2:15-18) Adam was alone at the time, Eve had not even been created yet; therefore, the prohibition could not have been a reference to sexual relations. Furthermore, the account tells us that it was when Adam was not with Eve that she "saw that the tree was good for food, and that it was a delight to the eyes, ... and she took of its fruit and ate, **then** she also gave some to her husband **when with her**, and he ate." (Genesis 3:6) Finally, after being removed from the Garden of Eden, Adam and Eve began having sexual relations and having children, and here is no record of them being criticized, condemned, or disciplined. (Genesis 4:1-2) So, Adam and Eve had sinned separately, not together.

Was Adam standing beside Eve when she had the conversation with the serpent, was deceived and chose to rebel against God? The Bible shows no indication that this is the case. Most translations make it appear as though that is the case, "she took of its fruit and ate, and she also **gave** some to **her husband who was with her**, and he ate."

The Hebrew verb translated "gave" is in the imperfect waw consecutive, as a result, it points to a temporal or logical sequence (usually called an "imperfect sequential"). Hence, a Bible translator or committee can translate the several occurrences of the waw, which tie together the chain of events in verse 6, with "and" as well as other transitional words, such as "subsequently," "then," "after that," afterward," and "so."

One has to ask themselves, would Adam have passively stood beside his wife Eve, listening to the conversation, between her and the serpent, as Satan spewed forth lies and malicious talk through this serpent, especially, especially, when Paul tells us explicitly that he was not deceived by the serpent? Supposedly, Adam just stood there and remained silent? Adam just chose not to interrupt the peddling of lies. Listen to the Bible scholar below; he actually believes this is reasonable.

The conversation with the serpent reveals that Adam had previously carried out his responsibilities as the head, informing her of the command not to eat from the tree. (Gen. 3:3) It seems far more likely that Satan, through the serpent ignored this headship, going after the newer person in the Garden of Eden, Eve, when she was alone. Eve later replied, "The serpent deceived me, and I ate." Unquestionably, the fruit that Adam and Eve ate separately did not represent sexual relations but rather was literal fruit that grew on a literal tree. Therefore, eating of the forbidden fruit would make an unfit and highly improbable symbol of sexual relations.

Was It Knowledge?

Some have claimed that the forbidden fruit was symbolic of having *knowledge* or *all knowledge.* Clearly, God had created both Adam and Eve with intellectual needs. They both were given basic knowledge and the capacity to grow in their knowledge and understanding of the world in which they were given. Both Adam and Even had already been taking in knowledge prior to their disobedience of eating the forbidden fruit. God himself had given them tasks to help them become more educated about creation. For example, they were given the task of naming all of the animals. It seems from Hebrew names for animals that they observed them for a while before naming them because their names were characteristic of their behaviors. (Genesis 2:19-20) Wasn't this being educated in zoology before we had zoology? Eve was by no means left in the dark, she evidenced that she to was educated about the one restriction of eating from the tree of good and evil. She was well aware of what was right and what was wrong, as well as the consequences for her actions. - Genesis 3:2-3.

Therefore, interpreting the original sin as sexual relations or knowledge is simply reading one's own interpretation into the text. The Bible can be difficult to understand at times because it was written in three ancient languages and culturally, we are 3,500 years removed. Even the apostle Peter said of the apostle Paul's letters, "there are some things in them that are hard to understand, which the ignorant and unstable twist to their own destruction, as they do the other Scriptures." (2 Pet. 3:16) In many cases, the Bible can interpret itself. There is nothing to indicate that the tree or the fruit was symbolic, both were literal and existed in the middle of the Garden of Eden. Thus, Adam and Eve were real historical person, who ate real fruit from a real tree.

Was It Disobedience?

The moment that Eve and then Adam ate this real forbidden fruit, they were disobeying God. Rebellion is disobedience or resistance to and defiance of what their sovereign God had commanded. The apostle Paul tells us in Romans 5:19 confirms the point: "For as through the one man's disobedience the many were made sinners." Therefore, the original sin was a disobedient act of rebellion against their sovereign Creator.

Sin may seem as though it is a simple small act of disobedience that comes across as extreme when we see the end result of suffering, old age, and death of untold billions. A footnote in *The New Jerusalem Bible* puts it this way: "This knowledge is a privilege which God reserves to himself and which man, by sinning, is to lay hands on, 3:5, 22. Hence it does not mean omniscience, which fallen man does not possess; nor is it moral discrimination, for unfallen man already had it and God could not refuse it to a rational being. It is the power of deciding for himself what is good and what is evil and of acting accordingly, a claim to complete moral independence by which man refuses to recognize his status as a created being. The first sin was an attack on God's sovereignty, a sin of pride." Yes, "the tree of the knowledge of good and evil" was God's way of teaching Adam and Eve that they were created and he alone had the right to set moral standards as to what was right and what was wrong. However, Adam and Eve rebelled and sought for themselves independence from God so that they could determine for themselves what was right and what was wrong. This called into question God's right to rule. Thus, God answered their disobedient rebellion by allowing man to rule himself. Through this object lesson, we can see that man was not designed to rule himself as it has been disastrous from the start. - Deuteronomy 32:5; Ecclesiastes 8:9.

Almost all translations translate Genesis 3:6 as follows.

Genesis 3:6 English Standard Version (ESV)	Genesis 3:6 Lexham English Bible (LEB)	Genesis 3:6 American Standard Version (ASV)	Genesis 3:6 New American Standard Bible (NASB)
6 So when the woman saw that the tree was good for food, and that it was a delight to the eyes, and that the tree was to be desired to make one wise, **she took of its fruit and ate, and she also gave some to her husband <u>who was with her</u>,** and he ate.	6 When the woman saw that the tree was good for food and that it was a delight to the eyes, and the tree was desirable to make one wise, then **she took from its fruit and she ate. And she gave it also to her husband <u>with her</u>,** and he ate.	6 And when the woman saw that the tree was good for food, and that it was a delight to the eyes, and that the tree was to be desired to make one wise, **she took of the fruit thereof, and did eat; and she gave also unto her husband with her**, and he did eat.	6 When the woman saw that the tree was good for food, and that it was a delight to the eyes, and that the tree was desirable to make one wise, **she took from its fruit and ate; and she gave also to her <u>husband</u> with her**, and he ate.

As you can see from these English translations, the plain sense of the text is, Adam was with her. This creates a real Bible difficulty. Before I delve into why, I will say that if almost all of the translations are in agreement, generally, this should be respected, and accepted. It is very unlikely that the very best Hebrew and Greek scholars of the past 100 years are all mistaken. Now, the difficulty arises because, if Eve and Adam were standing there before the tree of knowledge, as the serpent spoke to Eve, it means that Adam, the head, was very much involved in this process. Think as you read this commentary below, trying to rationalize how the situation played out, with the both being there.

Eve "was indeed deceived," but Adam "was not deceived." Of course, this cannot be taken absolutely. It must mean something on this order: Adam was not deceived in the manner in which Eve was deceived. See Gen. 3:4–6. She listened directly to Satan; he did not. She sinned before he did. She was the leader. He was the follower. She led when she should have followed;

that is, she led in the way of sin, when she should have followed in the path of righteousness.[61]

The reason for the difficulty is this; they are taking it as though Adam and Eve are standing before the tree of knowledge of good and evil, and the serpent, Satan, starts to speak to Eve. They carry on a conversation, with Adam only passively listening. Satan deceives Eve, but Adam is not deceived, yet he does not argue with the serpent, snatch the fruit from Eve, but rather just stands there letting Eve eat the fruit, knowing she will die. Really? I just cannot see how that can rationally be the case. I would argue that Eve was alone before Adam joined her.

Was Adam standing beside Eve when she had the conversation with the serpent, was deceived and chose to rebel against God? The Bible shows no indication that this is the case. The translations above make it appear as though that is the case, "she took of its fruit and ate, and she also **gave** some to **her husband who was with her,** and he ate."

The Hebrew verb translated "gave" is in the imperfect waw consecutive, as a result, it points to a temporal or logical sequence (usually called an "imperfect sequential"). Hence, a Bible translator or committee can translate the several occurrences of the waw, which tie together the chain of events in verse 6, with "and" as well as other transitional words, such as "subsequently," "then," "after that," afterward," and "so."

Genesis 3:6 English Standard Version (ESV)	**Genesis 3:6** Updated American Standard Version (UASV)
[6] So when the woman saw that the tree was good for food, **and** that it was a delight to the eyes, **and** that the tree was to be desired to make one wise, she took of its fruit **and** ate, **and** she also gave some to her husband who was with her, **and** he ate.	[6] So when the woman saw that the tree was good for food, **and** that it was a delight to the eyes, **and** that the tree was to be desirable to make one wise, **and** she took of its fruit **and** ate, *then* she also gave some to her husband when with her, **and** he ate.

One has to ask themselves, would Adam have passively stood beside his wife Eve, listening to the conversation, between her and the serpent, as Satan spewed forth lies and malicious talk through this serpent, especially, especially, when Paul tells us explicitly that he was not deceived by the serpent? Supposedly, Adam just stood there and remained silent? Adam just chose not to interrupt the peddling of lies. Listen to the Bible scholar below; he actually believes this is reasonable.

---

[61] William Hendriksen and Simon J. Kistemaker, vol. 4, Exposition of the Pastoral Epistles, New Testament Commentary, 110 (Grand Rapids: Baker Book House, 1953-2001).

Genesis 3:6 makes it clear that he was "with her" during the interchange with the serpent, but he remained silent. He should have interrupted. He should have chased the serpent off. And when it comes down to it, when he is offered the fruit himself, he eats it--no questions asked, no protests given. Adam and Eve together rebelled against their Creator, so they both suffer the horrible consequences.[62]

The conversation with the serpent reveals that Adam had previously carried out his responsibilities as the head, informing her of the command not to eat from the tree. (Gen. 3:3) It seems far more likely that Satan, through the serpent ignored this headship, going after the newer person in the Garden of Eden, Eve, when she was alone. Eve later replied, "The serpent deceived me, and I ate."

Let us assume that I am just mistaken, and it should be translated, "and she also gave some to her husband who was with her." Adam need not be clear on the other side of the Garden; he could have just been out of hearing range, and still have been with her. Suppose he was across the field, visually in sight, but still, out of hearing range, it could still be said he was with her. Husbands have you ever been in a huge store with your wife, like Wal-Mart, and at the same time you are on one side of the store (lawn-garden or automotive), and she is on the other side of the store. If you were to say you were **with your wife** at Wal-Mart, would that mean that you were necessarily standing right beside her? Say an issue came up in the store, so you walked over. The Garden of Eden was no small place, like a city park, but more like the size of a state park, possibly 18,000 acres of land and 3,000 acres of water. If Adam were in eyesight, but out of hearing range, it could still be said that he was with her. She could have called him over after her transgression, at which point, he demonstrated that his love for her was greater than that of his Creator, and so he ate.

Genesis 3:8 BDC: Did God speak directly to Adam?

Generally, in the Bible, when God had dealings with the human family, it was by means of an angel. (Gen. 16:7-11; 18:1-3, 22-26; 19:1; Judges 2:1-4; 6:11-16, 22; 13:15-22) The primary person in Scripture, who spoke and had dealings with humans, as a representative of the Father, Jehovah God, was his only only-begotten Son, appropriately called "the Word." (John 1:1) Therefore, while the Bible does not explicitly say, it was

---

[62] Longman III, Tremper (2005-05-12). How to Read Genesis (How to Read Series How to Read) (p. 111). Intervarsity Press - A. Kindle Edition.

very likely that God the Father spoke with Adam and Eve by means of "the Word." — Genesis 1:26-28; 2:16; 3:8-13.

GENESIS 3:16 OTBDC: Are women cursed by God?

Genesis 3:16 Updated American Standard Version (UASV)

[16] To the woman he said,

"I will surely **multiply your pain in childbearing; in pain** you shall bring forth children. **Your desire shall be for your husband,** and he shall **rule over you.**"

I will surely multiply your pain in childbearing; in pain you shall bring forth children: The grief, distress, and pain connected with giving birth is associated with the first sin. God revealed to Eve, after she had sinned, what the outcome would be as to childbearing. If she had continued to be faithful, God would have continued to bless her, and childbearing would have been a joy, for, "The blessing of Jehovah makes rich, and he adds no sorrow to it." (Proverbs 10:22) However, now, generally speaking, the woman is an imperfect human, missing the mark of perfection (sin), and her body brings forth pain. We have to understand that many times when God says he is doing some, it is actually something that he permits. Therefore, when God says that he is going to "**multiply your pain in childbearing; in pain,**" it really means that God is going to allow the bad results of her free will choice that she made under human perfection, as an object lesson for rejecting his sovereignty and choose to willfully sin against her creator.

While it is true that modern medicine can bring relief to the pain of pregnancy and childbearing and in some cases bringing about no pain whatsoever at all by good care and preparatory methods. Nevertheless, usually, childbirth continues as a physically distressing experience. – Genesis 35:16-20; Isaiah 26:17.

Your desire shall be for your husband, and he shall rule over you: The short answer is "no." Rather, it was "the great dragon was thrown down, the serpent of old who is called the devil and Satan, who deceives the whole inhabited earth," who had been cursed by God. (Revelation 12:9; Genesis 3:14) When God said that Adam would "rule over" his wife, God was not meaning that he approved of the bringing the woman under domination or control by man. (Genesis 3:16) He was merely foretelling the tragic outcome of sin on the first husband and wife.

Consequently, the abuse of women that have been so common over the past six millennia is a direct outcome of the sinful nature of humans, not of God's will and purposes. The Bible in no way supports the idea that women must be controlled or dominated by men in order to atone for the original sin. – Romans 5:12.

EDWARD D. ANDREWS

GENESIS 3:17 OTBDC: How is it that the ground would be cursed for Adam, and for how long?

Genesis 3:17 Updated American Standard Version (UASV)

[17] And to Adam he said,

"Because you have listened to the voice of your wife and have eaten of the tree of which I commanded you, 'You shall not eat of it,' cursed is the ground because of you; in toil you shall eat of it all the days of your life;

The curse that Jehovah God had placed on the ground meant that cultivation was going to be a far greater task than it would have been had Adam not sinned. Lamech, Noah's father, in connection with the thorns and thistles, expresses this level of the curse, "the painful toil of our hands." (Gen 5:29) The curse was lifted after the flood, at which time God blessed his faithful servants Noah and his sons. (Gen 9:1) Jehovah gave Noah and his family a good start, reissued the command to multiply and fill the earth (Gen 13:10), and placed under man's power the animal and plant realms, with no handicapping curse on the earth: "I will never again curse the soil because of man." However, take note that the work of cultivating the entire earth given to Adam was not contained within that given to Noah. This suggests that there would not be an earth-wide paradise accomplished by imperfect man, just because the curse was lifted. – Gen. 1:28; 6:17; 8:21; 9:1-17.

Genesis 3:19-21 BDC: Will Adam and Eve Receive a Resurrection?

Genesis 3:19-21 Updated American Standard Version (UASV)

¹⁹ By the sweat of your face you shall eat bread, till you return to the ground, for out of it you were taken; for you are dust, and to dust you shall return."

²⁰ Now the man called his wife's name Eve,⁶³ because she was the mother of all living. ²¹ And Jehovah God made for Adam and for his wife garments of skins and clothed them.

The conclusion below will be drawn from silence and cannot be taken dogmatically. It is inferential only, and the final answer will have to be one that we seldom like, 'we will have to wait and see.' However, just because something is drawn from silence does not necessarily mean it is not true. We have absolutely no record that Jesus ever bathed, but we can be most certain that he did. It is certainly true that both Adam and Eve attempted to sidestep their responsibility of eating from the forbidden tree. Adam blamed Eve, while Eve blamed the serpent. However, both did not deny that they had actually violated the command.

Jehovah has said that if you eat from this tree, "you shall surely die." (Gen. 2:17) That was the explicit punishment, death. Their sentence was to "suffer the punishment of eternal destruction." (2 Thess. 1:9) The reason that this could be said is, justice required death, with no provision for anything else at the time that they were given the command. It does not seem fair that a Just God, in his command, would not include additional punishments of Eve's difficulty in childbirth and Adam's struggle to get the earth to respond to his care if they were a part of the original provision. It seems that the extra penalty for Eve ("I will greatly multiply thy pain and thy conception; in pain thou shalt bring forth children"), and for Adam ("cursed is the ground for thy sake; in toil shalt thou eat of it all the days of thy life"); where a means to move the two to repentance. Do the extra penalties, which were not part of the original punishment, for eating the forbidden fruit, mean that Jehovah was going to forgive them after they paid the price that he had laid down? The Apostle Paul said at Romans 6:7, "he that hath died is justified from sin."

Just as humankind is under the condemnation of death, because we are sinners; as Romans 5:12 informs us, "Therefore, as through one man sin entered into the world, and death through sin; and so death passed unto all men, for that all sinned." Thus, it would seem that Adam and Eve could be afforded this as well, being chastised beyond the original punishment,

---

⁶³ Personal name meaning "life." (Heb., *Chawwah*)

because of Jehovah's love for them. In fact, he did not give them this additional punishment, until after he informed them of the hope held out to all of the humankind, the hope of a coming seed. (Gen. 3:15) Discipline by God is because of his love, and it always starts as a means of correction, this extra chastisement was a constructive reminder of their unfaithfulness to him and their need to return and repent. We have no knowledge that they ever returned to God, or that they did not for that matter.

It is very much possible that when Jehovah God clothed and protected the first human couple, he informed them, of the coming seed, Jesus Christ (Gen. 3:15), who would crush the head of the serpent (Satan), and "give his life as a ransom for many." (Matt 20:28) It would seem that God must have informed Adam of the atoning value of the blood sacrifice as well. Otherwise, we are in a difficulty, as to how Abel, Adam's second son, acquired this knowledge. – Genesis 4:4.

Both Cain and Abel brought their offering to the altar individually. This means that Adam had no priestly function. The vegetable offering of Cain would have been displeasing to Adam because it was displeasing to Jehovah. Cain's offering lacked the atoning blood. (Gen. 4:5) On the other hand, Jehovah was well pleased with Abel's blood atoning sacrifice of "the firstborn of his flock and of their fat portions." – Genesis 4:4.

Some may argue that Adam and Eve were perfect, and this would indicate that they had no excuse for their rebellious act, which means that they willfully and knowingly sinned against God under perfection, like the blasphemy against the "Spirit" that Jesus spoke of, forfeiting any hope of a resurrection. (Matt. 12:32; Heb. 6:4-6) They would point out maybe that we in our imperfection are prone, inclined, leaned toward sin, while Adam and Eve were prone, inclined and leaned toward good. However, the Christian can find himself, because of the ransom sacrifice of Christ, in an approved standing before God. There are allowances made for his imperfection, which means, he has a righteous standing before God. (Ps 103:8-14) Thus, if we were to put them on a scale, Adam would not have needed any allowance for his standing before Jehovah, while God graciously gives imperfect man that has a genuine, active faith in Christ some counterweights undeservedly so, to offset and give him his standing before Jehovah.

In the end, we must say that there is no conclusive answer to this question. One should offer both arguments and allow the listener to decide for themselves where they stand. The other option is to be neutral and not commit to either position, choosing to wait and see, as God is a God of mercy, love, and justice, and will do the right thing. In conclusion, it is difficult for this writer to believe that Adam and Eve spent 930 years and did not repair their relationship with their Father.

Genesis 4:3-4 BDC: Why was Cain's offering unacceptable to God?

There are two aspects of Cain's offering, which found him unapproved before God: **(1)** his attitude and **(2)** the type of offering.

Eventually, Cain and Abel came before God with their offerings. "Cain brought to Jehovah an offering of the fruit of the ground." (Gen. 4:3) "Also brought of the firstlings of his flock and of their fat portions." (Gen. 4:4) It is likely that both Cain and Abel were close to 100 years old at the time, as Adam was 130 years old when he fathered his third son, Seth. – Genesis 4:25; 5:3.

Genesis 4:3-4 Updated American Standard Version (UASV)

3 And in the course of time[64] Cain brought to Jehovah an offering of the fruit of the ground. 4 And Abel, he also brought of the firstlings of his flock and of their fat portions. And Jehovah had regard for Abel and his offering; 5 but for Cain and his offering he had no regard. So Cain was very angry, and his face fell.[65]

We can establish that the two sons became aware of their sinful state and sought our God's favor. How they garnered this knowledge is guesswork, but it is likely by way of the father, Adam. Adam likely informed them about the coming seed and the hope that lie before humankind.[66] Therefore, it seems that they had given some thought to their condition and stand before God, and realized that they needed to try to atone for their sinful condition. The Bible does not inform us just how much time they had given to this need before they started to offer a sacrifice. Rather, God chose to convey the more important aspect, each one's heart attitude, which gives us an inside look at their thinking.

Some scholars have suggested that Eve felt that Cain was the "seed" of the Genesis 3:15 prophecy that would destroy the serpent, "she conceived and bore Cain, and said, 'I have gotten a man with the help of Jehovah.'" (Gen. 4:1) It might be that Cain shared in this belief and had begun to think too much of himself, and thus the haughty spirit. If this is the case, he was very mistaken. His brother Abel had a whole other spirit, as he offered his sacrifice in faith, "By faith Abel offered to God a more acceptable sacrifice

---

64 Lit., *of days*
65 Or, his countenance fell
66 Adam's family must have received God's revelation about the necessity of sacrifice to create and maintain fellowship with God. The background to this was probably the sacrifice that God performed to provide the clothing to cover Adam and Eve's shame (see Gen. 3:21). Anders, Max; Gangel, Kenneth; Bramer, Stephen J. (2003-04-01). Holman Old Testament Commentary – Genesis: 1 (p. 56). Holman Reference. Kindle Edition.

than Cain, through which he was commended as righteous, God commending him by accepting his gifts." – Hebrews 11:4.

It seems that Abel was capable of discerning the need for blood to be involved in the atoning sacrifice, while Cain was not, or simply did not care. Therefore, it was the heart attitude of Cain as well. Consequently, "but on Cain and his offering he did not look with favor. So Cain was very angry, and his face was downcast." (Gen 4:5, NIV) It may well be that Cain had little regard for the atoning sacrifice, giving it little thought, going through the motions of the act only. However, as later biblical history would show, Jehovah God is not one to be satisfied with formal worship. Cain had developed a bad heart attitude, and Jehovah well knew that his motives were not sincere. The way Cain reacted to the evaluation of his sacrifice only evidenced what Jehovah already knew. Instead of seeking to improve the situation, "Cain was very angry, and his face fell." (Gen. 4:5) As you read the rest of the account, it will become clearer as to the type of temperament Cain had before Jehovah God.

Genesis 4:6-16 Updated American Standard Version (UASV)

⁶ Then Jehovah said to Cain, "Why are you angry, and why has your face fallen? ⁷ If you do well, will there not be a lifting up?⁶⁷ And if you do not do well, sin is crouching at the door. Its desire is for you, but you must rule over it."

⁸ Cain said to Abel his brother. And it came about when they were in the field, that Cain rose up against Abel his brother and killed him.

⁹ Then Jehovah⁶⁸ said to Cain, "Where is Abel your brother?" And he said, "I do not know. Am I my brother's keeper?" ¹⁰ He said, "What have you done? The voice of your brother's blood is crying to me from the ground. ¹¹ Now you are cursed from the ground, which has opened its mouth to receive your brother's blood from your hand. ¹² When you cultivate the ground, it will no longer yield its strength to you; you will be a fugitive and a wanderer on the earth." ¹³ Cain said to Jehovah, "My punishment is greater than I can bear! ¹⁴ Behold, you have driven me today away from the ground, and from your face I shall be hidden. I shall be a fugitive and a wanderer on the earth, and whoever finds me will kill me." ¹⁵ So Jehovah said to him, "Therefore whoever kills Cain, vengeance will be taken on him sevenfold." And Jehovah put a mark on Cain, so that no one finding him would slay him.

---

⁶⁷ This is a shortening of the Hebrew idiom "to lift up the face," which means "to accept" favorably
⁶⁸ The Tetragrammaton, God's personal name, יהוה (*JHVH/YHWH*), which is found in the Hebrew Old Testament 6,828 times.

[16] Then Cain went out from the presence of Jehovah, and dwelt in the land of Nod,[69] east of Eden.

---

[69] I.e. wandering

GENESIS 3:24 OTBDC: Why Has God Permitted Wickedness and Suffering?

Genesis 3:24 Updated American Standard Version (UASV)

²⁴ So he drove the man out, and at the east of the garden of Eden he placed the cherubim and a flaming sword that turned every way to guard the way to the tree of life.

"God has morally sufficient reasons for permitting the evil and suffering in the world." – William Lane Craig

That *morally sufficient reason* lies below.

"The significant issue that drove me to Agnosticism [Bible Scholar Dr. Bart D. Ehrman is now an Agnostic] has to do not with the Bible, but with the pain and suffering in the world." He writes, "I eventually found it impossible to explain the evil so rampant among us—whether in terms of genocides (which continue), unspeakable human cruelty, war, disease, hurricanes, tsunamis, mudslides, the starvation of millions of innocent children, you name it—if there was a good and loving God who was actively involved in this world." *Misquoting Jesus* (p. 248)

As you will see below, Ehrman's issue is simply a matter of starting with the wrong assumption. **Point One:** He starts with 'if God is a God of love, who has the power to fix anything, how can there have been such horrific pain and suffering in imperfection over the last 6,000 years?' **Point Two:** He also likely begins with the premise that 'God is responsible for everything that happens.' If one starts with the wrong assumption, there is no doubt that he will reach the wrong conclusion(s). **Point One** is dealt with below, but let it be said that Ehrman is looking through the binoculars from the opposite end, the big side through the small. When we do that, we get a narrow, focused outlook. God looks through the binoculars the correct way and can see the big picture. Ehrman can only see but a fraction and a moment of time, 70 – 80 years, while God has seen everything that has happened over these past 6,000 plus years in the greatest of detail and can see what the outcome would be if he had handled things in a variety of ways.

Point Two is certainly one reason suffering and evil is often misunderstood. God is responsible for everything, but not always directly. If he started the human race, and we end up with what we now have, in essence, he is responsible. Just as parents, who have a child are similarly responsible for the child committing murder 21 years into his life, because they procreated and gave birth to the child. The mother and father are indirectly responsible. King David commits adultery with Bathsheba and has her husband Uriah killed to cover things up, and impregnates

Bathsheba, but the adulterine child, who remains nameless, died. Is God responsible for the death of that child? We can answer yes and no to that question. He is responsible in two ways: **(1)** He created humankind, so there would have been no affair, murder, adulterine child if he had not. **(2)** He did not step in and save the child when he had the power to do so. However, he is not directly responsible, because he did not make King David and Bathsheba commit the acts that led to the child being born, nor did he bring an illness on the adulterine child, he just did not move in to protect the child, in a time that had a high rate of infant deaths.

The reason people think that God does not care about us is the words of some religious leaders, which have made them, feel this way. When tragedy strikes, what do some pastors and Bible scholars often say? When 9/11 took place, with thousands dying in the twin towers of New York, many ministers said: "It was God's will. God must have had some good reason for doing this." When religious leaders make such comments or similar ones, they are actually blaming God for the bad things that happened. Yet, the disciple James wrote, "Let no one say when he is tempted, 'I am being tempted by God,' for God cannot be tempted with evil, and he himself tempts no one." (James 1:13) God never directly causes what is bad. Indeed, "far be it from God that he should do wickedness, and from the Almighty that he should do wrong." Job 34:10.

The history of humans has been inundated with pain and suffering on an unprecedented scale, much of which they have brought on themselves. The problem/question that has plagued many persons is, 'why if there is a loving God, would he allow it to start with, and worse still, why allow it to go on for over 6,000 years?' Some apologist scholars have struggled to answer this question, because they are over analyzing, as opposed to just looking for the answer in God's Word. Therefore, if we are to answer this question, we must go back to Adam and Eve at the time of the first sin. Many have read this account, but I will list the texts as a refresher.

Genesis 2:17 Updated American Standard Version (UASV)

[17] but from the tree of the knowledge of good and evil you shall not eat,[70] for in the day that you eat from it you shall surely die."[71]

Genesis 3:1-5 Updated American Standard Version (UASV)

[1] Now the serpent was more crafty than any beast of the field which Jehovah God had made. And he said to the woman, "Did God actually say, 'You[72] shall not eat of any tree in the garden'?" [2] And the woman said to

---

[70] Lit *eat from it*
[71] Lit *dying you* [singular] *shall die.* Heb *moth tamuth;* the first reference to death in the Scriptures
[72] In Hebrew *you* is plural in verses 1–5

the serpent, "From the fruit of the trees of the garden we may eat, [3] but from the tree that is in the midst of the garden, God said, 'You shall not eat from it, nor shall you touch it, lest you die.'" [4] And the serpent said to the woman, "You shall not surely die. [5] For God knows that when you eat of it your eyes will be opened, and you will be like God, knowing good and evil." knowing good and evil.

Later Bible texts establish Satan the Devil as the one using a serpent as his mouthpiece like a ventriloquist would a dummy. Anyway, take note that Satan contradicts the clear statement that God made to Adam at Genesis 2:17, "you will not surely die." Backing up a little, we see Satan asking an inferential question, "Did God actually say, 'You shall not eat of any tree in the garden'?" First, he is overstating what he knows to be true, not "any tree," just one tree. Second, Satan is inferring, 'I can't believe that God would say . . . how dare he say such.' Notice too that Eve has been told so thoroughly about the tree that she even goes beyond what Adam told her, not just that you 'do not eat from it,' no, 'you do not even touch it!' Then, Satan out and out lied and slandered God as a liar, saying that 'they would not die.' To make matters much worse, he infers that God is withholding good from them, and by rebelling they would be better off, being like God, 'knowing good and bad.' This latter point is not knowledge of; it is the self-sovereignty of choosing good and bad for oneself and act of rebellion for created creatures. What was symbolized by the tree is well expressed in a footnote on Genesis 2:17, in The Jerusalem Bible (1966):

> This knowledge is a privilege which God reserves to himself and which man, by sinning, is to lay hands on, 3:5, 22. Hence it does not mean omniscience, which fallen man does not possess; nor is it moral discrimination, for unfallen man already had it and God could not refuse it to a rational being. It is the power of deciding for himself what is good and what is evil and of acting accordingly, a claim to complete moral independence by which man refuses to recognize his status as a created being. The first sin was an attack on God's sovereignty, a sin of pride.

The Issues at Hand

(1) Satan called God a liar and said he was not to be trusted, as to the life or death issue.

(2) Satan's challenge, therefore, took into question the right and legitimacy of God's rightful place as the Universal Sovereign.

(3) Satan also suggested that people would remain obedient to God only as long as their submitting to God was to their benefit.

(4) Satan all but said that humankind was able to walk on his own, there being no need for dependence on God.

(5) Satan argued that man could be like God, choosing for himself what is right and wrong.

(6) Satan claimed that God's way of ruling was not in the best interests of humans, and they could do better without God.

Job 1:6-11 Updated American Standard Version (UASV)

6 Now there was a day when the sons of God came to present themselves before Jehovah, and Satan also came among them. 7 Jehovah said to Satan, "From where do you come?" Then Satan answered Jehovah and said, "From roaming about on the earth and walking around on it." 8 Jehovah said to Satan, "Have you considered my servant Job? For there is no one like him on the earth, a blameless and upright man, fearing God and turning away from evil." 9 Then Satan answered Jehovah, "Does Job fear God for nothing? 10 Have you not made a hedge about him and his house and all that he has, on every side? You have blessed the work of his hands, and his possessions have increased in the land. 11 But put forth your hand now and touch all that he has; he will surely curse you to your face."

Job 2:4-5 Updated American Standard Version (UASV)

4 Satan answered Jehovah and said, "Skin for skin! Yes, all that a man has he will give for his life. 5 However, put forth your hand now, and touch his bone and his flesh; he will curse you to your face."

This general reference to "a man," as opposed to explicitly naming Job, is suggesting that all men [and women] will only obey God when things are good, but when the slightest difficulty arises, he will not obey. If you were put to the test, would you prove your love for your heavenly Father and show that you preferred His rule to that of any other?

God Settles the Issues

There is one thing that Satan did not challenge, namely, the power of God. Satan did not suggest that God was unable to destroy him as an opposer. However, he did challenge God's way of ruling, not His right to rule. Therefore, a moral issue must be settled.

An illustration of how God chose to deal with the issue can be demonstrated in human terms. A neighbor down the street slandered a man, who had a son and daughter. The slanderer said that he was not a good father, i.e., he withheld good from his children and was so overbearing, to the point of being abusive. The slanderer stated that the children would be better off without their father. He further argued that the children had no real love for their father and only obeyed him because of the food and shelter. How should the father deal with these false, i.e., slanderous accusations? If he were to go down the road and pummel the slanderer, it would only validate the lies, making the neighbors believe the accuser is telling the truth.

The answer lies within his family as they can serve as his witnesses. (Pro 27:11; Isa 43:10) If the children stay obedient and grow to be successful adults, turning out to be loving, caring, honest people with spotless character, it proves the accusations false. If the children accept the lies and rebel and grow up to be despicable people, it just further validates that they would have been better off by staying with the father. This is how God chose to deal with the issues. The issues that were raised must be settled beyond all reasonable doubt.

If God had destroyed the rebellious three: Satan, Adam, and Eve; he would not have resolved the issues of

(1) Whether man could walk on his own,

(2) if he would be better off without his Creator,

(3) if God's rulership were not best, and

(4) if God were hiding good from man.

(5) In addition, there was an audience of untold billions of angelic spirit creatures looking on.

If God destroyed without settling things, these spirit persons would be following God out of dreadful fear, not love, fear of displeasing God. Moreover, say He did kill them, and start over, and ten thousand years down the road (with billions of humans now on earth), the issues were raised again, He would have to destroy billions of people again, and again, and again all throughout time, until these issues were laid to rest.

What God has done is, allow time to pass, and the issues to be resolved. Man thought he was better off without God, and could walk on his own. In addition, man has attempted every kind of rulership imaginable, and one must ask, 'have they proven themselves better than rulership under the sovereignty of their Creator?' (Proverbs 1:30-33; Isaiah 59:4, 8) Sadly, the issues must be taken up to the brink of destroying man. (Rev 11:18) Otherwise, the argument would be that if given enough time, they could have turned things around. If man goes up to the point of destroying himself and Armageddon comes at the last minute, it will have set a case law, solved the issue, and the Bible can serve as the example forever. If the issues of God's sovereignty or the loyalty of His created creatures, angelic or human, is ever questioned again, we would have the Holy Bible that will serve as a law established based on previous verdicts of not guilty, please see below.

What Have the Results Been?

(1) God does not cause evil and suffering. Romans 9:14.

(2) The fact that God has allowed evil, pain and suffering has shown that independence from God has not brought about a better world. Jeremiah 8:5, 6, 9.

(3) God's permission of evil, pain, and suffering has also proved that Satan has not been able to turn all humans away from God. Exodus 9:16; 1 Samuel 12:22; Hebrews 12:1.

(4) The fact that God has permitted evil, pain, and suffering to continue has provided proof that only God, the Creator, has the capability and the right to rule over humankind for their eternal blessing and happiness. Ecclesiastes 8:9.

(5) Satan has been the god of this world since the sin in Eden (over 6,000 years), and how has that worked out for man, and what has been the result of man's course of independence from God and his rule? Matthew 4:8-9; John 16:11; 2 Corinthians 4:3-4; 1 John 5:19; Psalm 127:1.

Satan's impact on the earth's activities has carried with it conflict, evil and death, and his rulership has been by means of deception, power and his own self-interest. He has demonstrated himself an unfit ruler of everything. Therefore, God is now completely vindicated in putting an end to this corrupted rebel along with all who have shared in his evil deeds. – Romans 16:20.

God has tolerated evil, sickness, pain, suffering and death until our day in order to resolve all the issues raised by Satan. We are self-centered in thinking that this has only pained us. Imagine that you are holding a rope on a sinking ship that 20 other men, women, and children are clinging to, when your child loses her grip and falls into the ocean. You can hold the rope, saving 20 people, or you can let go and attempt to rescue your daughter. God has been watching the suffering of billions from the day of Adam and Eve's sin. Moreover, it has been His great love for us, which causes Him to cling to the rope of issues, saving us from a future of repeated issues. Nevertheless, he will not allow this evil to remain forever. He has set a fixed time when He will end this wicked system of Satan's rule.

Daniel 11:27 Updated American Standard Version (UASV)

[27] As for both kings, their heart will be inclined to do what is evil, and they will speak lies to each other at the same table; but it will not succeed, for the end is still to come <u>at the appointed time</u>.

Unlike what many people of the world may think (the world that lies in the hands of Satan), being obedient to God is not difficult. We simply must set our pride aside and accept that the wisdom of God is so far greater than our own and accept that He has worked for the good of obedient humankind, as He loves each one of us.

Matthew 7:21 Updated American Standard Version (UASV)

[21] "Not everyone who says to me, 'Lord, Lord,' will enter the kingdom of heaven, but the one who does the will of my Father who is in heaven.

1 John 2:15-17 Updated American Standard Version (UASV)

[15] Do not love the world or the things in the world. If anyone loves the world, the love of the Father is not in him. [16] For all that is in the world, the lust of the flesh and the lust of the eyes and the boastful pride of life, is not from the Father, but is from the world. [17] The world is passing away, and its lusts; but the one who does the will of God remains forever.

As Christians, there is a love we must not have. We must 'not love the world or anything in it.' Instead, we need to keep from becoming infected by the corruption of unrighteous human society that is alienated from God and must not breathe in its mental disposition or be moved by its sinful dominant attitude. (Ephesians 2:1, 2; James 1:27) If we were to have the views of those in the world that are in opposition to God, "the love of the Father" would not be in us. (James 4:4)

Was Satan Punished?

Yes.

COMMON QUESTION: Why did God not destroy the Satan, Adam, and Eve right away?

I would follow up with what would have happened if God had chosen that path. Hundreds of billions of angels with free will were watching, and they knew of the issues raised. What would their love of God have been like if God did not address the issues raised? Was Satan, right? Was God lying? Would free will creatures, spirit and humans, be better off? Will God just destroy us over anything? First, the spirit creatures would have followed God out of dreadful fear, rather than fear of displeasing the one they loved so much up to that point, like a child to a parent. Second, what happens if the issue is raised a hundred thousand years after a restart and there are 30 billion perfect humans on the planet? Would God simply destroy everyone again and start over. Do we think it wise that he does this reboot every time or was it not better that he settled the issue once and for all?

POINT: Satan raised Issues of sovereignty in the Garden of Eden.

POINT: Can humans walk on their own; do they really need their Creator? Are they better off without God?

POINT: Was God lying and withholding?

When a teenager becomes a rebel in our house, we have a choice: (1) severe punishment or (2) teach them an object lesson.

HUMANS AND ANGELS are a created product no different than a car coming off of an assembly line, i.e., (1) they owe their existence to their creator and (2) they were created to function based on the design of the creator. If we take a ford escort and treat it like a heavy-duty four-wheel drive truck and go off roading (not what the car was designed to do), what will happen?

God wisely chose to teach both angels and humans an object lesson. Neither was designed to walk on their own. Both angel and human were given relative freedom (under the sovereignty of God), not absolute freedom. They were not designed to choose what is right and what is wrong on their own. They were given God's moral standards by way of an internal conscience. How can we tell a rebel that we do not have absolute freedom, we are better off under the umbrella of our creator's sovereignty, we cannot walk on our own? They will just reject it as a rebel teenager would.

OBJECT LESSON: We let them learn from their choice, no matter how painful it is, and hard love means that we do not step in until the lesson is fully learned. Humankind was essentially told, "Oh, you think you can walk on your own, well go ahead, we will see how that works out." After six-thousand-years, God could actually use a common saying among young people today: "How is that absolute freedom working out for you?"

When will the lesson fully be learned? Humankind will walk right up to the very edge of the cliff of killing themselves, actually falling over, when God will step in and stop the object lesson. To stop it anytime before, will cause doubts. If it had been stopped a century ago, the argument would have been; God simply stepped in before we got to the scientific age because he knew we were going to find true peace and security, along with something to give us eternal life. However, if humanity has actually fallen over the edge of the cliff and the destruction of us is definite, and God steps in, no argument can be raised, the object lesson is learned.

Why Was Satan Not Kicked Out of Heaven Right Away?

Satan stayed in his realm, just as humans stayed in theirs. God changed nothing right away because he would have been accused of adjusting the pieces on the chessboard to get the desired outcome, i.e., cheating. When will Satan be kicked out of heaven? Satan and the Demons lost access to the person of God long age, and they lost some of their powers, such as being able to materialize in human form, like they did when they took human women for themselves at the flood, producing the Nephilim.

Satan would be thrown to the earth very shortly before the end of his age of rulership, when "he knows that his time is short." (Rev 12:9-12) This, then, means that Satan will be thrown from heaven likely sometime before the Great Tribulation and Christ's return. Revelation 12:12 says, "'Therefore, rejoice, O heavens and you who dwell in them! But woe to you, O earth and sea, for the devil has come down to you in great wrath because he knows that his time is short!'"

Notice that it is at a time, when "Satan knows that his time is short!" What comes next for Satan? He will be abyssed, thrown into a super-maximum-security prison for a thousand years (for lack of a better way to explain it) while Jesus fixes all that Satan done. After the thousand years, he will be let loose for a little while, and he will tempt perfect humans, and sadly some will fall away. In the end, Satan and those humans will be destroyed, and Jesus will hand the kingdom back over to the father.

Genesis 4:8, 12-13 BDC: Why did Cain not receive capital punishment for the murder he committed?

Genesis 4:8 Updated American Standard Version (UASV)

[8] Cain said to Abel his brother. "Let us go out into the field."[73] And it came about when they were in the field, that Cain rose up against Abel his brother and killed him.

Genesis 9:6 Updated American Standard Version (UASV)

[6] "Whoever sheds man's blood,
By man his blood shall be shed,
For in the image of God
he made man.

Exodus 21:12 Updated American Standard Version (UASV)

[12] "He who strikes a man so that he dies shall be put to death.

As can be seen from the above, the penalty for willfully taking the life of another is the death penalty. We see from the account concerning Cain that he not only did not receive the death penalty for murdering his brother Abel, but he was given protection from anyone seeking to avenge that murder. – Genesis 4:15.

At first glance, this may seem like inconsistency on the part of Jehovah's justice, but it is not. There are multiple reasons as to why Cain did not receive the death penalty. At the time of this murder, God had not established the death penalty for the murder of another. (Rom 13:1-4) It was only after, "the LORD saw that the wickedness of man was great in the earth and that every intention of the thoughts of his heart was only evil continually." (Gen 6:5) After the destruction of the Nephilim and wicked man by means of the flood, did God say, ""Whoever sheds the blood of man, by man shall his blood be shed ..." – Genesis 9:6.

Jehovah is the giver of life and death, and he rightly chose to give Cain a life sentence of banishment. (Deut. 32:39) However, God did express his thoughts that Cain was worthy of death. Jehovah said, "What have you done? The voice of your brother's blood is crying to me from the ground." (Gen. 4:10) Even Cain himself knew that death was the possibility, and asked Jehovah for protection. Cain said to the Jehovah, "My punishment is greater than I can bear. Behold, you have driven me today away from the ground, and from your face, I shall be hidden. I shall be a fugitive and a wanderer on the earth, and whoever finds me will kill me." (Gen. 4:13-14) In addition, the death penalty then was made known as an option, for

---

[73] **Genesis 4:8**: SP LXX It Syr inserts these bracketed words; Vg, "Let us go outdoors"; MT omits; some MSS and editions have an interval here.

the taking of a life, as Jehovah said, "If anyone kills Cain, vengeance shall be taken on him sevenfold." (Gen. 4:15) Therefore, due to mitigating circumstances, Cain is the exception to the rule, and cannot be used against the justice of the death penalty that was to become a part of human law after the flood.

GENESIS 4:15 OTBDC: How did God "put a mark on Cain"?

Genesis 4:15 Updated American Standard Version (UASV)

[15] So Jehovah said to him, "Therefore whoever kills Cain, vengeance will be taken on him sevenfold." And Jehovah put a mark on Cain, so that no one finding him would slay him.

The Hebrew for "a mark" is (*'ôt* sign), which has a semantic range that is very broad,[74] can means "a sign," (Gen. 1:14; 4:15), "a banner," "standard," or "flag" (Num. 2:2; Ps 74:4), as well as "a miracle, wonder, sign," that is, a mighty act of God that serves as a message of wonder or to instill referential fear. (Ex. 4:8-9, 17; Nu 14:11, 22; Deut. 4:34; 6:22; Jos 24:17; Jdg 6:17; Neh. 9:10; 2Ki 20:8, 9; Ps. 74:9; 78:43; 105:27; 135:9; Isa 38:7; Jer. 32:20, 21) On this K. A. Mathews writes,

> This "mark of Cain," as it is popularly known, has proven to be a seedbed for confusion (v. 15b). "Mark" is the common word for "sign" (*'ōt);* the exact nature of the sign or its place on the body ("on Cain") is unknown. One Jewish tradition pointed to Cain himself as the "sign" who served to admonish others to repentance (*Gen. Rab.* 22.12). In effect this has become true for later generations, if not his own, for Cain the man has become a token of sin's fruit and divine retribution (1 John 3:12; Jude 11). Although "sign" is used figuratively in several passages (e.g., Exod 13:9; Deut 6:8; 11:18), the only parallel is Ezek 9:4, where certain men receive a mark on the forehead. But even there it is in an extended vision in which it only has symbolic force. What is important here is its purpose: "so that no one who found him would kill him" (v. 15). "Mark" in our passage is not a sign of the "curse"; in fact, it assures Cain's safety rather than acts as a reproach. The mark in Ezekiel's vision had the same effect; it distinguished those who bore the brand and gave them protection.[75]

The Bible does not say exactly what this mark was, but it is highly unlikely that it was a physical mark on his person. Such a mark would be meaningless centuries later when thousands of people were living before the flood. The sign was likely a verbal decree made by Jehovah to Adam and Eve, which would have become an oral tradition that would have been passed down from generation to generation, avoiding the murder of Cain

---

[74] Ernst Jenni and Claus Westermann, *Theological Lexicon of the Old Testament* (Peabody, MA: Hendrickson Publishers, 1997), 67.

[75] K. A. Mathews, *Genesis 1-11:26*, vol. 1A, The New American Commentary (Nashville: Broadman & Holman Publishers, 1996), 278.

for the sake of revenge. It would seem that at least one Jewish tradition was seeing this view similarly, i.e., it was not a physical mark. While this seems the preferred understanding, one cannot be dogmatic, it is simply inferred from what seems reasonable and logical, as well as in harmony with the use of the Hebrew.

Genesis 4:17 OTBDC: Where did Cain get his wife?

Genesis 4:17 Updated American Standard Version (UASV)

[17] Cain had sexual relations[76] with his wife and she conceived, and gave birth to Enoch; and he built a city, and called the name of the city Enoch, after the name of his son, Enoch.

Genesis 3:20 Updated American Standard Version (UASV)

[20] Now the man called his wife's name Eve, because she was the mother of all living.

Here we are just setting up the situation, and as you can see, all humans came to be the offspring of Adam and Eve.

Genesis 5:3-4 Updated American Standard Version (UASV)

[3] When Adam had lived one hundred and thirty years, he became[77] the father of a son in his own likeness, according to his image, and named him Seth. [4] Then the days of Adam after he became the father of Seth were eight hundred years, and he had other sons and daughters.

As you can see, aside from Cain and Abel, there was Seth, as well as "other sons and daughters." Therefore, one of Adam's daughters must have married Cain. In fact, they lived for centuries; it could have even been his niece. We must keep in mind that these are the immediate descendants of Adam and Eve; therefore, they would have been closer to perfection. Their condition of good health would be far beyond the healthiest person living today; so, there would have been no chance of passing on defects, as would be the case even in the Time of Abraham, when they were still living almost 200 years. This is the reason you find Jehovah God forbidding incest 2.500 years later in the Mosaic Law.

Genesis 4:16-17 Updated American Standard Version (USV)

[16] Then Cain went out from the presence of Jehovah, and dwelt in the land of Nod,[78] east of Eden.

[17] Cain had sexual relations[79] with his wife and she conceived, and gave birth to Enoch; and he built a city, and called the name of the city Enoch, after the name of his son, Enoch.

---

[76] Lit *knew*
[77] Lit *begot*
[78] I.e. wandering
[79] Lit *knew*

Please note that Cain met his wife before he fled to another land. She was not from some other family. However, it was there that they had relations, and fathered a son.

GENESIS 4:26 OTBDC: Exactly when did the worship of God begin?

Genesis 4:26 Updated American Standard Version (UASV)

26 To Seth, to him also a son was born; and he called his name Enosh. At that time men began to call upon the name of Jehovah.

It is here that we are expressly told, "To Seth, to him also a son was born, and he called his name Enosh. At that time men began to call upon the name of Jehovah." (Gen. 4:26) This is in the days of Enosh, the son of Seth, the third son of Adam and Eve. However, over 105 years earlier before the birth of Enosh, you have Abel offering sacrifices to God in faithful worship. (Gen. 4:3-4) Is this not a historical error? No.

Obviously, in the days of Enosh, we are not talking about calling on the name of Jehovah in faith and pure worship as Abel had done. Some Hebrew scholars have offered that it should read, "began profanely," or "then profanation began." In reference to Enosh's day, the Targum of Onkelos says, "then in his days the sons of men desisted from praying in the Name of the Lord." The Targum[80] of Jonathan says, "That was the generation in whose days they began to err, and to make themselves idols, and surnamed their idols by the Name of the Word of the Lord." Rashi an influential Jewish Bible Commentator from the twelfth century C.E. says, "Then was there profanation in calling on the Name of the Lord." Furthermore, if the purity of worship was begun in the days of Enosh, instead of profanation in calling on the Name of Jehovah, what "ungodliness" did Enoch; "the seventh from Adam" have to prophesy about in Jude 14-15? It could be that men misused the name of Jehovah by applying it to themselves, or other men, approaching God through these ones in worship. Alternatively, it could be that they applied Jehovah's name on idol objects.

---

80 The Targum is an Aramaic translation of part of the Bible.

How Could Satan, Adam, and Eve Have Sinned If They Were Perfect?

One member of an apologetic Facebook group expressed his inability to understand the often stated, "if God allows man to choose ... that means man's will is stronger."

The reason you do not understand it is that it's nonsensical. This is the way of Calvinism and the once saved always saved, eternal security, predestined lost persons. So, if a Father of a child allows his child over time as the child matures to make the child's own decisions on certain things, that means the child's will is stronger? Really? When God gave Adam and Eve free will, the ability to choose, he also gave them a perfect conscience that gave them the capacity to make perfect decisions. However, the principle in James 1:14 that if you entertain or cultivate a bad idea, you will eventually give way to it applied to them as well.

James 1:14-15 Updated American Standard Version (UASV)

[14] But each one is tempted when he is carried away and enticed by his own desire.[81] [15] Then the desire when it has conceived gives birth to sin, and sin when it is fully grown brings forth death.

Did Satan, Adam, and Eve need to have to make all their decisions right after being created in order to qualify as a perfect creation?

To suggest such a thing would be saying that they had no free will, they had no choice. God did not create Satan, Adam, and Eve to make automatic programmed decisions. God gave them freedom of choice to obey Him out of love, or they could love themselves more and be disobedient. (Deut. 11:1; 1 John 5:3) The qualities of a created being with no ability to choose and being created with free will (the capacity to choose) are not the same. The former is a robot, the latter is a human. Therefore, because we have had sin enter into the world, it means that God gave spirit creatures and humans free will, the ability to choose between right and wrong, to make moral decisions. For example, to eat from the tree of knowledge was bad, to not eat from it was good. This is the way spirit persons and humans were designed, the inability to make morally right decisions would have indicated imperfection: failure, weakness, shortcoming.

Did Satan, Adam, and Eve need to have to make all their decisions right after being created in order to qualify as a perfect creation?

---

[81] Or "own lust"

To suggest such a thing would be saying that they had no free will, they had no choice. God did not create Satan, Adam, and Eve to make automatic programmed decisions. God gave them freedom of choice to obey Him out of love, or they could love themselves more and be disobedient. (Deut. 11:1; 1 John 5:3) The qualities of a created being with no ability to choose and being created with free will (the capacity to choose) are not the same. The former is a robot, the latter is a human. Therefore, because we have had sin enter into the world, it means that God gave spirit creatures and humans free will, the ability to choose between right and wrong, to make moral decisions. For example, to eat from the tree of knowledge was bad, to not eat from it was good. This is the way spirit persons and humans were designed, the inability to make morally right decisions would have indicated imperfection: failure, weakness, shortcoming.

Would perfection mean that Satan, Adam, and Eve were not able to do wrong?

Think it through logically, if God had not given Satan, Adam and Eve free will, there would be no wickedness. If there was no such thing as free will, and Satan, Adam and Eve were created without it, they could not have ever sinned unless God chose for them to sin, making God words that Hitler. But God has given his intelligent creatures free will, the capacity to choose to obey God out of love for Him or to disobey Him out of love for self. (Deut. 30:19-20; Josh. 24:15) If God had created the angels, Adam, and Eve without free will; then, God would have created the perfect robots and they would have done exactly what he wanted them to do. Even if God had created Adam and Eve as perfect robots (lacking free will), they would not have been perfect humans.

How is it those perfect spirit persons and humans could commit acts of sin?

Perfection does not mean one can abuse the creation and there not be dire results. If perfect humans smoked cigarettes, it would still cause damage, it would just take longer. If perfect humans ate unhealthy food, their bodies would still pay the price. Thus, the moment God created spirit persons and humans and gave them an internal moral code, there would be things that would be good and things that would be bad. Satan allowed a bad thought to enter his mind and instead of dismissing it, he entertained it. When Satan approached Eve, she too entertained the bad thoughts, which caused moral decline, unholiness. Again, James 1:14-15 explains: "But each one is tempted when he is carried away and enticed by his own desire. Then the desire when it has conceived gives birth to sin, and sin when it is fully grown brings forth death."

Consider Eve's words about a tree that she likely saw thousands of times, "So when the woman saw that the tree was good for food, and that **it was a delight to the eyes**, and that **the tree was to be desirable** to make one wise, and she took of its fruit and ate, then she also gave some to her husband when with her, and he ate." (Gen. 3:1-6) The eyes are a window to the heart, the seat of motivation. The wrong desires if Eve grew as she listened to Satan, as he used the serpent to tempt her with bad thoughts. Adam then showed more love for his wife than God. Both could have rejected the wrong thoughts. Both entertain and cultivated selfish desires, resulting in sin.

EDWARD D. ANDREWS

View of Bible Difficulties

By R. A. Torrey

Updated By Edward D. Andrews

Every careful student and every thoughtful reader of the Bible finds that the words of the Apostle Peter concerning the Scriptures, that there are some things in them hard to be understood is true. The apostle Peter says of Paul's letters, "as also in all his [Paul's] letters, speaking in them of these things, in which are some things **hard to understand**, which the untaught and unstable distort, as they do also the rest of the Scriptures, to their own destruction." (2 Peter 3:16, UASV) If this were true of Peter, how much more so of us 2,000 years removed, of a different language and culture? This is abundantly true for us! Who of us has not found things in the Bible that have puzzled us, yes, that in our early Christian experience have led us to question whether the Bible was, after all, the Word of God? We find some things in the Bible, which it seems impossible to reconcile with other things in the Bible. We find some things, which seem incompatible with the thought that the whole Bible is of divine origin and absolutely inerrant.

It is not wise to attempt to conceal the fact that these difficulties exist. It is the part of wisdom, as well as of honesty, to frankly face them and consider them.

What shall we say concerning these difficulties that every thoughtful student will eventually encounter?

The first thing we have to say about these difficulties in the Bible is that from the very nature of the case *difficulties are to be expected.*

Some people are surprised and staggered because there are difficulties in the Bible. For my part, I would be more surprised and staggered if there were not. What is the Bible? It is a revelation of the mind and will and character and being of an infinitely great, perfectly wise and absolutely holy God. God, Himself is the Author of this revelation. However, one would ask, to who specifically is the revelation made? To men, to finite beings who are imperfect in intellectual development and consequently in knowledge, and who are imperfect in character and consequently in spiritual discernment. The wisest man measured on the scale of eternity is only a babe, and the holiest man compared with God is only an infant in moral development.

Therefore, there must from the very necessities of the case, be difficulties in such a revelation from such a source made to such persons. In addition, when the finite is attempting to understand the infinite, there is bound to be a difficulty. When the ignorant contemplate the utterances of one perfect in knowledge, there must be many things hard to be understood, and some things, which to their immature and inaccurate minds appear absurd. When beings whose moral judgments as to the hatefulness of sin and as to the awfulness of the penalty that it demands, listen to the demands of an absolutely holy Being, they are bound to be staggered at some of His demands, and when they consider His dealings, they are bound to be staggered at some of His dealings. These dealings will appear too severe, too stern, and too harsh.

It is plain that there must be difficulties for us in such a revelation as the Bible has proved to be. If someone should hand me a book that was as simple to me as the multiplication table, and say, "This is the Word of God; in it He has revealed His whole will and wisdom," I should shake my head and say, "I cannot believe it; that is too easy to be a perfect revelation of infinite wisdom." There must be in any complete revelation of God's mind and will and character and being, things hard for the beginner to understand; and the wisest and best of us are but beginners.

The second thing to be said about these difficulties is that a difficulty in a doctrine, or a grave objection to a doctrine, does not in any way prove the doctrine untrue.

Many people think that it does. If they come across some difficulty in the way of believing in the divine origin and absolute inerrancy and infallibility of the Bible, they at once conclude that the doctrine is exploded. That is very illogical. They should stop a moment and think, and learn to be reasonable and fair.

There is scarcely a doctrine in science generally believed today, that has not had some great difficulty in the way of its acceptance.

When the Copernican theory (the earth revolves around the sun and not vice versa), now so universally accepted, was first proclaimed, it encountered a very grave difficulty. If this theory were true, the planet Venus should have phases as the moon has, but the best glass could discover no phases then in existence. However, the positive argument for the theory was so strong that it was accepted in spite of this apparently unanswerable objection. When a more powerful glass was made, it was found that Venus had phases after all. The whole difficulty arose, as most; all of those in the Bible arise, from man's ignorance of some of the facts in the case.

The nebular hypothesis (the formation of the solar system) is commonly accepted in the scientific world today. Nevertheless, when this theory was first announced, and for a long time afterward, the movements of the planet Uranus could not be reconciled with the theory. Uranus seemed to move in just the opposite direction from that in which it was thought it ought to move in accordance with the demands of the theory.

However, the positive arguments for the theory were so strong that it was accepted in spite of the inexplicable movements of Uranus.

If we apply to Bible study the commonsense logic recognized in every department of science (with the exception of Biblical criticism, if that be a science), then we must demand that if the positive proof of a theory is conclusive, it must be believed by rational men in spite of any number of difficulties in minor details. He is a shallow thinker who gives up a well-attested truth because there are some apparent facts, which he cannot reconcile with that truth. In addition, he is a very shallow Bible scholar who gives up his belief in the divine origin and inerrancy of the Bible because there are some supposed facts that he cannot reconcile with that doctrine. There are in the theological world today many shallow thinkers of that kind.

The third thing to be said about the difficulties in the Bible is: there are many more, and much greater, difficulties in the way of the doctrine that holds the Bible to be of human origin, and hence fallible, than there are in the way of the doctrine that holds the Bible to be of divine origin, and hence infallible.

Turning the Tables

Oftentimes a man will put forth some difficulty and say, "How do you explain that, if the Bible is the Word of God?" You may not be able to answer him satisfactorily. Then he thinks he has you cornered. Not at all, turn on him, and ask him, "How do you account for the fulfilled prophecies of the Bible if it is of human origin? How do you account for the marvelous unity of the Book? How do you account for its inexhaustible depth? How do you account for its unique power in lifting men up to God?" For every insignificant objection he can bring to your view of the Bible, you can bring very many more deeply significant objections to his view of the Bible. Moreover, any candid man who desires to know and obey the truth will have no difficulty in deciding between the two views.

Some time ago a young man, who was of a bright mind and unusually well read in skeptical, critical, and agnostic literature, told me he had given the matter a great deal of candid and careful thought, and as a result, he could not believe the Bible was of divine origin.

I asked him, "Why not?"

He pointed to a certain teaching of the Bible that he could not and would not believe to be true.

I replied, "Suppose for a moment that I could not answer that specific difficulty; that would not prove that the Bible is not of divine origin. I can bring you many things far more difficult to account for on the hypothesis that the Bible is not of divine origin than on the hypothesis that the Bible is of divine origin. You cannot deny the fact of fulfilled prophecy. How do you account for it if the Bible is not God's Word? You cannot shut eyes to the marvelous unity of the sixty-six books of the Bible, written under such divergent circumstances and at periods of time so remote from one another. How do you account for it if God is not the real Author of the Book back of the forty or more human authors? You cannot deny that the Bible has a power—to save men from sin, to bring men peace and hope and joy, to lift men up to God—that all other books taken together do not possess. How do you account for it if the Bible is not the Word of God in a sense that no other book is the Word of God?"

The objector did not answer. The difficulties that confront one who denies that the Bible is of divine origin and authority are far more numerous and vastly more weighty than those which confront the one who believes it to be of divine origin and authority.

The fourth thing to be said about the difficulties in the Bible is: *the fact that you cannot solve a difficulty does not prove it cannot be solved, and the fact that you cannot answer an objection does not prove at all that it cannot be answered.*

It is remarkable how often we overlook this very evident fact. There are many, who meet a difficulty in the Bible and give it a little thought and can see no possible solution, at once jump to the conclusion that a solution is impossible, and so they give up their faith in the inerrancy of the Bible and in its divine origin. Any man should have a sufficient amount of modesty, being so limited in knowledge, to say, "Though I see no possible solution to this difficulty, someone a little wiser than I might easily find one."

If we would only bear in mind that we do not know everything, and there are a great many things that we cannot solve now which we could very easily solve if we only knew a little more, it would save us from all this foolishness. We ought never to forget that there may be a very easy solution to infinite wisdom even for that which to our finite wisdom—or ignorance—appears unsolvable. What would we think of a beginner in algebra who, having tried in vain for half an hour to solve a difficult problem, declared that there was no possible solution to the problem because he could find none!

A man of unusual experience and ability one day left his work and drove a long distance to see me, as he was in great uneasiness of mind because he had discovered what he believed to be a flat contradiction in the Bible. He had lain awake all night thinking about it. It had defied all his attempts at reconciliation, but when he had fully stated the case to me, in very few moments I showed him a very simple and satisfactory solution of the difficulty. He went away with a happy heart. Nevertheless, why had it not occurred to him at the outset that, though it appeared impossible to him to find a solution, after all, someone else might easily discover a solution? He supposed that the difficulty was an entirely new one, but it was one that had been faced and answered long before either he or I were born.

The fifth thing to be said about the difficulties in the Bible is that *the seeming defects of the Book are exceedingly insignificant when put in comparison with its many and marvelous areas of excellence.*

It certainly reveals great perversity of both mind and heart that men spend so much time focusing on and exaggerating such insignificant points, which they consider defects in the Bible, and pass absolutely unnoticed the incomparable beauties and wonders that adorn and glorify almost every page. This is even taking place in some prominent institutions of learning, where men are supposed to be taught to appreciate and understand the Bible and where they are sent to be trained to preach its truth to others. These institutions are spending much more time on minute and insignificant points that seem to point toward an entirely human origin of the Bible than is spent on studying and understanding and admiring the unparalleled glories that make this Book stand apart from all other books in the world. What would we think of any man who in studying some great masterpiece of art concentrated his whole attention upon what looked like a flyspeck in the corner? A large proportion of the much boasted about "critical study of the Bible" is a laborious and scholarly investigation of supposed flyspecks. The man who is **not** willing to squander the major portion of his time in this intellectualized investigation of flyspecks but prefers to devote it to the study of the unrivaled beauties and majestic splendors of the Book is counted in some quarters as not being "scholarly and up to date."

The sixth thing to be said about the difficulties in the Bible is that *they have far more weight with superficial readers than with profound students.*

Take a man like Colonel Ingersoll, who was very ignorant of the real contents and meaning of the Bible, or that class of modern preachers who read the Bible for the most part for the sole purpose of finding texts to serve as pegs to hang their own ideas. To such superficial readers of the Bible these difficulties seem of immense importance, but to one who has learned to meditate upon the Word of God day and night they have scarcely any weight at all. That rare man of God, George Müller, who had carefully studied the Bible from beginning to end more than one hundred times, was not disturbed by any difficulties he encountered; but to the man who is reading it through for the first or second time there are many things that perplex and stagger.

The seventh thing to be said about the difficulties in the Bible is that *they rapidly disappear upon careful and prayerful study.*

How many things there are in the Bible that once puzzled and staggered us, but which have since been perfectly cleared up and no longer present any difficulty whatever! Every year of study finds these difficulties disappear more and more rapidly. At first, they go by ones, and then by twos, and then by dozens, and then by scores. Is it not reasonable then to suppose that the difficulties that remain will all disappear upon further study?

EDWARD D. ANDREWS

Some Types of Bible Difficulties

By R. A. Torrey

Updated by Edward D. Andrews

All the difficulties found in the Bible can be included under ten general headings:

The Text from which our English Bible was Translated

No one, as far as I know, holds that the English translation of the Bible is absolutely infallible and inerrant. The doctrine held by many is that the Scriptures as originally given were absolutely infallible and inerrant, and that our English translation is a *substantially accurate* rendering of the Scriptures as originally given.

We do not possess the original manuscripts of the Bible. These original manuscripts were copied many times with great care and exactness, but naturally, some errors crept into the copies that were made. We now possess so many good copies that by comparing one with another, we can tell with great precision just what the original text was. Indeed, for all practical purposes the original text is now settled.

Update: After Torrey's death in 1928, we have made the extremely important discovery over 100 papyrus manuscripts that date before 300 C.E. Quite a few date to the second century, with one small fragment being dated to about 125 C.E. The modern textual scholar can now say with certainty that we have establish the Greek New Testament to a ninety-nine percent reflect of the originally publish book(s). Moreover, we have more than 100 English translations today, with many of them being a very good representation of the Hebrew and Greek in English: NASB, ESB, HCSB, LEB, and others. **Edward D. Andrews**

There is not one important doctrine, which hangs upon any doubtful reading of the text. However, when our Authorized Version (KJV) was published in 1611, some of the best manuscripts were not within reach of the translators, and the science of textual criticism was not so well understood as it is today, and so the translation was made from an imperfect text. Not a few of the apparent difficulties in the Bible arise from this source.

For example, we are told in John 5:4 that "an angel went down at a certain season into the pool, and troubled the water: whosoever then first after the troubling of the water stepped in was made whole of whatsoever disease he had." This statement for many reasons seems improbable and difficult to believe, but upon investigation, we find that it is all a mistake of the copyist. Some early copyist, reading John's account, added in the margin his explanation of the healing properties of this intermittent medicinal spring. A late copyist embodied this marginal note in the body of the text, and so it came to be handed down and got into the Authorized Version (KJV). Very properly, it has been omitted from the Revised Version.

Note: It is omitted from almost all of our modern-day translations as well, with the exception of the NASB and the HCSB, which retained it out of esteem to the KJV. **Edward D. Andrews**

The discrepancies in figures in different accounts of the same events as, for example, the differences in the ages of some of the kings as given in the text of Kings and Chronicles, doubtless arise from the same cause, errors of copyists. Such an error in the matter of figures would be very easy to make, as in the Hebrew; letters, and letters that appear very much alike have a very different value as figures denote numbers. For example, the first letter in the Hebrew alphabet denotes one, and with two little points above it, no larger than flyspecks, it denotes a thousand. The twenty-third or last letter of the Hebrew alphabet denotes four hundred, but the eighth letter of the Hebrew alphabet that looks very much like it and could be easily mistaken for it, denotes eight. A very slight error of the copyist would therefore make an utter change in figures. The remarkable thing when one contemplates the facts in the case is that so few errors of this kind have been made.

Inaccurate Translations

For example, in Matthew 12:40 Jonah is spoken of as being in "the whale's belly." Many a skeptic has made a mockery over the thought of a whale with the peculiar construction of its mouth and throat swallowing a man. However, if the skeptic had only taken the trouble to look the matter up, he would have found the word translated "whale" really means "sea monster" [or great fish] without any definition as to the character of the sea monster. We will take this up more in detail in considering the story of Jonah. Therefore, the whole difficulty arose from the translator's mistake and the skeptic's ignorance. Many skeptics today are so densely ignorant of matters clearly understood by many Sunday school children that they are still harping in the name of scholarship on this supposed error in the Bible.

False Interpretations of the Bible

What the Bible teaches is one thing, and what men interpret it to mean is oftentimes something widely different. Many difficulties that we have with the Bible arise not from what the Bible actually says, but from what men interpret it to mean.

A striking illustration of this is found in Genesis 1. If we were to take the interpretation put upon this chapter by many, it would indeed be difficult to reconcile it with much that modern science regards as established. However, the difficulty is not with what Genesis 1 says, but with the interpretation put upon it. There is no contradiction whatever between what is really proven by science and what is really said in Genesis 1.

Another difficulty of the same character is with Jesus' statement that He would be three days and three nights in the heart of the earth. Many interpreters would have us believe that He died Friday and rose early Sunday morning, and the time between these two is far from being three days and three nights. However, it is a matter of biblical interpretation, and the trouble is not with what the Bible actually says, but with the interpretation that men put upon the Bible. We will take this matter up at length below by Edward D. Andrews.

Matthew 12:40 How many days was Jesus in the tomb?

Some argue for three days, based on Jesus' words,

Matthew 12:40 English Standard Version (ESV)

⁴⁰ For just as Jonah was three days and three nights in the belly of the great fish, so will the Son of Man be three days and three nights in the heart of the earth.

This would seem to suggest a full 72 hours. However, we should not set aside similar expressions that may allow us to get at the intent of the words. Many times in Scripture, three days does not always mean a full 72 hours of three days. For example, look at the words of Rehoboam,

1 Kings 12:5, 12 English Standard Version (ESV)

⁵ He said to them, "Go away for three days, then come again to me." So the people went away. ¹² So Jeroboam and all the people came to Rehoboam the third day, as the king said, "Come to me again the third day."

You see that the king told the people to go away for three days, and then return to him. But you also will notice that they returned on the third day, which was not a full 72 hours of three days. Now, consider what Jesus said of himself, something that Scripture repeatedly says,

Luke 24:46 English Standard Version (ESV)

⁴⁶ and said to them, "Thus it is written, that the Christ should suffer and **on the third day** rise from the dead

Now, if he had remained in the grave for a full 72 hours of three days, it mean that he would have been raised on the fourth day. Jewish days ran from sundown to sundown. Jesus died on Friday afternoon about 3:00 p.m., Nisan 14, 33 C.E.

- Jesus' death Friday Nisan 14, about 3:00 p.m. (Matt 27:31-56; Mk 15:20-41; Lu 23:26-49; Jn 19:16-30)

- Jesus was in Tomb before sundown Friday evening (Matt 27:57-61; Mk 15:42-47; Lu 23:50-56; Jn 19:31-42)

- Jesus in tomb all of Nisan 15ᵗʰ from sundown Friday to sundown Saturday, which began Nisan 16 (Matt 27:62-66)

- Jesus resurrected early Sunday morning of Nisan 16ᵗʰ (Matt 28:1; Mk 16:1; Lu 24:1; Jn 20:1)

Therefore, Jesus was dead and in the tomb for at least a period of time on Friday Nisan 14, was still in the tomb during the course of the whole day of Nisan 15, and spent the nighttime hours of Nisan 16 in the tomb.

- Now after the Sabbath, toward the dawn of the first day of the week, Mary Magdalene and the other Mary went to see the tomb. (Matt 28:1)

- When the Sabbath was past, Mary Magdalene, Mary the mother of James, and Salome bought spices, so that they might go and anoint him. (Mk 16:1)

- But on the first day of the week, at early dawn, they went to the tomb, taking the spices they had prepared. (Lu 24:1)

- Now on the first day of the week Mary Magdalene came to the tomb early, while it was still dark, and saw that the stone had been taken away from the tomb. (Jn 20:1)

Certain women came to the tomb on Sunday morning, it was still dark, he had already been resurrected. Thus, Jesus had been in the tomb for parts of three days.

A Wrong Conception of the Bible

Many think that when we say the Bible is the Word of God, of divine origin and authority, we mean that God is the speaker in every utterance it contains; but this is not what is meant at all. Oftentimes, it simply records what others say, i.e., what good men say, what bad men say, what inspired men say, what uninspired men say, what angels and demons say, and even what the devil says. The record of what they said is from God and absolutely true, but what those other persons are recorded as saying may be true or may not be true. It is true that they said it, but what they said may not be true.

For example, the devil is recorded in Genesis 3:4 as saying, "You will not surely die." It is true that the devil said it, but what the devil said is not true, but an infamous lie that shipwrecked our race. That the devil said it is God's Word, but what the devil said is not God's word but the devil's word. It is God's Word that this was the devil's word.

Very many careless readers of the Bible do not notice who is talking, God, good men, bad men, inspired men, uninspired men, angels or devil. They will tear a verse right out of its context regardless of the speaker and say, "There, God said that." However, God said nothing of the kind. God's Word says that the devil said it or a bad man said it or a good man said it or an inspired man said it, or an uninspired man said it, or an angel said it. What God says is true, namely, that the devil said it, or a bad man, or a good man, or an inspired man, or an uninspired man, or an angel. However, what they said may or may not be true.

It is very common to hear men quote what Eliphaz, Bildad or Zophar said to Job as if it were necessarily God's own words because it is recorded in the Bible, in spite of the fact that God disavowed their teaching and said to them, "you have not spoken of me what is right" (Job 42:7). It is true that these men said the thing that God records them as saying, but often they gave the truth a twist and said what is not right. A very large share of our difficulties thus arises from not noticing who is speaking. The Bible always tells us, and we should always note it. Below, under the subheadings of "the Case of Job" and "The Comforters" Andrews demonstrates how the erroneous interpretations come about.

The Case of Job

What we have covered thus far will help us understand one of the more complex books of the Bible, the book of Job.

Job was a "blameless and upright man, who fears God and turns away from evil." Job was living the happy life; he had seven sons and the daughters. He was a wealthy landowner. "He possessed 7,000 sheep, 3,000 camels, 500 yoke of oxen, and 500 female donkeys, and very many servants, so that this man was the greatest of all the people of the east." (1:3) Even so, he is not a materialistic person; he was simply following a proverb like the above, 'if you work hard, your efforts will be blessed.'

Job 1:13-19; 2:7-8 English Standard Version (ESV)

¹³Now there was a day when his sons and daughters were eating and drinking wine in their oldest brother's house, ¹⁴and there came a messenger to Job and said, "The oxen were plowing and the donkeys feeding beside them, ¹⁵and the Sabeans fell upon them and took them and struck down the servants with the edge of the sword, and I alone have escaped to tell you." ¹⁶While he was yet speaking, there came another and said, "The fire of God fell from heaven and burned up the sheep and the servants and consumed them, and I alone have escaped to tell you." ¹⁷While he was yet speaking, there came another and said, "The Chaldeans formed three groups and made a raid on the camels and took them and struck down the servants with the edge of the sword, and I alone have escaped to tell you." ¹⁸While he was yet speaking, there came another and said, "Your sons and daughters were eating and drinking wine in their oldest brother's house, ¹⁹and behold, a great wind came across the wilderness and struck the four corners of the house, and it fell upon the young people, and they are dead, and I alone have escaped to tell you." ²:⁷So Satan went out from the presence of the LORD and struck Job with loathsome sores from the sole of his foot to the crown of his head. ⁸And he took a piece of broken pottery with which to scrape himself while he sat in the ashes.

The Comforters

Job 4:7-8 English Standard Version (ESV)

⁷"Remember: who that was innocent ever perished? Or where were the upright cut off? ⁸As I have seen, those who plow iniquity and sow trouble reap the same.

Eliphaz in an attempt at dealing with Job's atrocities assumes Job's tragedies are a result of his own actions. Eliphaz has reasoned wrong by taking a proverb and making it an absolute. In essence, he asks Job, 'do those that are innocent die? When have those that live a righteous life been destroyed?' Eliphaz goes on by saying, 'my experience suggests that it is those who are doing wrong and entertain bad that will get back what they gave out.' In other words, Eliphaz is assuming that only the wicked reap bad times.

Job 5:15 English Standard Version (ESV)

¹⁵But he saves the needy from the sword of their mouth and from the hand of the mighty.

Eliphaz again assumes that Job is at fault. Eliphaz is assuming that it was Job's great riches, which were ill gotten, and this is why he is suffering. Is Eliphaz's statement wrong in and of itself? No, God does rescue the poor from the oppressive, by their following his counsel on the right way to live. However, this is no absolute; saying all who live by God's will and purposes will never be mistreated. Moreover, the whole idea is misplaced, in that maybe Job is the rich oppressor and this is his punishment from God.

Job 8:3-6 English Standard Version (ESV)

³Does God pervert justice? Or does the Almighty pervert the right? ⁴If your children have sinned against him, he has delivered them into the hand of their transgression.⁵If you will seek God and plead with the Almighty for mercy, ⁶if you are pure and upright, surely then he will rouse himself for you and restore your rightful habitation.

Bildad too is stating true statements, but in absolute terms that are misplaced when it comes to Job, or anyone. Certainly, God does not pervert justice. Therefore, Bildad is right on that, but his application and understanding is what is twisted, as he assumes that children died because they had sinned, and justice was being meted out to them. Again, in verse 5-6, we have a true thought, in that if one is in an impure state, and turns to God with pleadings, he will restore them. However, in verses 5-6, Bildad is assuming that Job is unrighteous, because he sees that proverb as an absolute.

As can be seen from the above, one must be aware that proverbs are not absolutes, but are general truths. True enough, there are likely a couple of exceptions to this rule, but that would not negate this rule, and approach of correct interpretation of proverbs.

In the Psalms, we have sometimes, what God said to man and that is always true; but on the other hand, we often have what man said to God, and that may or may not be true. Sometimes, and far oftener than most of us see, it is the voice of the speaker's personal vengeance or despair. This vengeance may be and often is prophetic, but it may be the wronged man committing his cause to Him to whom vengeance belongs (Romans 12:19), and we are not obliged to defend all that he said. In the Psalms, we have even a record of what the fool said, "There is no God" (Psalm 14:1). Now it is true that the fool said it, but the fool lied when he said it. It is God's Word that the fool said it, but what God reports the fool as saying is not God's own word at all but the fool's own word.

Therefore, in studying our Bible, if God is the speaker we must believe what He says. If an inspired man is the speaker, we must believe what he says. If an uninspired man is the speaker, we must judge for ourselves, it is perhaps true, perhaps false. If it is the devil who is speaking, we do well to remember that he was a liar from the beginning; but even the devil may tell the truth sometimes.

The Language in Which the Bible was Written

The Bible is a book of all ages and for all kinds of people, and therefore it was written in the language that continues the same and is understood by all, the language of the common people and of appearances. It was not written in the terminology of science.

Thus, for example, what occurred at the Battle of Gibeon (Joshua 10:12–14) was described in the way it appeared to those who saw it, and the way in which it would be understood by those who read about it. There is no talk about the refraction of the sun's rays, and so forth, but the sun is said to have *"stood still"* (or tarried) in the midst of heaven. It is one of the perfections of the Bible that it was not written in the terminology of modern science. If it had been, it would never have been understood until the present day, and even now it would be understood only by a few. Furthermore, as science and its terminology are constantly changing, the Bible if written in the terminology of the science of today would be out of date in a few years; but being written in just the language chosen, it has proved the Book for all ages, all lands and all conditions of men.

Other difficulties from the language in which the Bible was written arise from the fact that large portions of the Bible are poetical and are written in the language of poetry, the language of feeling, passion, imagination and figure. Now if a man is hopelessly matter-of-fact, he will inevitably find difficulties with these poetical portions of the inspired Word.

For example, in Psalm 18 we have a marvelous description of a thunderstorm, but let the dull, matter-of-fact fellow get hold of that, for example, verse 8: "Smoke went up from his nostrils, and devouring fire from his mouth; glowing coals flamed forth from him," and he will be head over heels in difficulty at once. However, the trouble is not with the Bible, but with his own stupid, thickheaded plainness.

Our Defective Knowledge of the History, Geography and Usages of Bible Times

For example, in Acts 13:7 Luke speaks of "the deputy" (more accurately "the proconsul," see English Standard Version) of Cyprus. Roman provinces were of two classes, imperial and senatorial. The ruler of the imperial provinces was called a propraetor, of a senatorial province a proconsul. Up to a comparatively recent date, according to the best information we had, Cyprus was an imperial province and therefore its ruler would be a propraetor, but Luke calls him a proconsul. This certainly seemed like a clear case of error on Luke's part, and even the conservative commentators felt forced to admit that Luke was in slight error, and the destructive critics were delighted to find this "mistake." Further and more thorough investigation has brought to light the fact that just at the time of which Luke wrote the senate had made an exchange with the emperor whereby Cyprus had become a senatorial province, and therefore its ruler was a proconsul. Luke was right after all, and the literary critics were themselves in error.

Repeatedly further researches and discoveries, geographical, historical and archaeological, have vindicated the Bible and put to shame its critics. For example, the book of Daniel has naturally been one of the books that unbelievers and destructive critics have most hated. One of their strongest arguments against its authenticity and truthfulness was that such a person as Belshazzar was unknown to history, that all historians agreed that Nabonidus was the last king of Babylon, and that he was absent from the city when it was captured. Therefore, Belshazzar must be a purely mythical character, and the whole story legendary and not historical. Their argument seemed very strong. In fact, it seemed unanswerable. However, Sir H. Rawlinson discovered at Mugheir and other Chaldean sites clay cylinders on which Belshazzar (Belsaruzar) is named by Nabonidus as his eldest son. Doubtless he reigned as regent in the city during his father's absence, an indication of which we have in his proposal to make Daniel third ruler in the kingdom (Daniel 5:16). He himself being second ruler in the kingdom, Daniel would be next to him. So the Bible was vindicated again.

The critics asserted most positively that Moses could not have written the Pentateuch because writing was unknown in his day. However, recent discoveries have proved beyond a question that writing far antedates the time of Moses. So the critics have been compelled to give up their argument, though they have had the bad grace to hold on stubbornly to their conclusion.

The Ignorance of Conditions under Which Books Were Written and Commands Given

For example, to one ignorant of the conditions, God's commands to Israel as to the extermination of the Canaanites seem cruel and horrible. However, when one understands the moral condition to which these nations had sunk, the utter hopelessness of reclaiming them and the weakness of the Israelites themselves, their extermination seems to have been an act of mercy to all succeeding generations and to themselves.

The Many-Sidedness of the Bible

The broadest-minded man is one-sided, but the truth is many-sided, and the Bible is all-sided. Therefore, to our narrow thought one part of the Bible seems to contradict another.

For example, religious men as a rule are either Calvinistic or Arminian in their mental makeup. In addition, some portions of the Bible are decidedly Calvinistic and present great difficulties to the Arminian type of mind, while other portions are decidedly Arminian and present difficulties to the Calvinistic type of mind. However, both sides are true. Many men in our day are broad-minded enough to be able to grasp at the same time the Calvinistic side of the truth and the Arminian side of the truth; but some are not, so the Bible perplexes, puzzles and bewilders them. The trouble is not with the Bible, but with their own lack of capacity for comprehensive thought.

Expansion: These schools of doctrinal positions are initially established religious leaders and their followers, such as John Calvin and Jacob Arminius. There are even more, such as the Lutheran, from Martin Luther, The Wesleyan, from John Wesley, and the Mennonites, from Menno Simons, and Society of Friends (Quakers) under George Fox. Actually, I would disagree with Torrey here, I believe that he should have used his earlier point of argument, it boils down to the truth of the Bible as being absolute, but man may misinterpret that truth. Therefore, it will lay concealed until discovered. This misinterpretation does not refute the infallibility or inerrancy of Scripture. Actually, doctrine plays no part in inerrancy of Scripture. Whether one believes the earth was created in six literal 24-hour days, or six creative periods called days, has no impact on the doctrine of inerrancy. The Bible is inerrant and one of those interpretations is wrong and the other is correct. This has to do with the person interpreting the Bible, not the inerrancy of the Bible. **Edward D. Andrews**

Therefore, Paul seems to contradict James, and James seems sometimes to contradict Paul; and what Paul says in one place seems to contradict what he says in another place. However, the whole trouble is that our narrow minds cannot take in God's large truth.

The Bible has to do with the Infinite, and our Minds are Finite

It is necessarily difficult to put the facts of infinite being into the limited capacity of our finite intelligence, just as it is difficult to put the ocean into a pint cup. To this class of difficulties belong those connected with the Bible doctrines of the Trinity and of the divine-human nature of Christ. To those who forget that God is infinite, the doctrine of the Trinity seems like the mathematical monstrosity of making one equal three. However, when one bears in mind that the doctrine of the Trinity is an attempt to put into forms of finite thought the facts of infinite being, and into material forms of expression the facts of the spirit, the difficulties vanish. The simplicity of the Unitarian conception of God arises from its shallowness.

The Dullness of our Spiritual Perception

The man who is farthest advanced spiritually is still so immature that he cannot expect to see everything yet as an absolutely holy God sees it, unless he takes it upon simple faith in Him. To this class of difficulties belong those connected with the Bible doctrine of eternal punishment. It often seems to us as if this doctrine cannot be true, must not be true, but the whole difficulty arises from the fact that we are still so blind spiritually that we have no adequate conception of the awfulness of sin, and especially of the awfulness of the sin of rejecting the infinitely glorious Son of God. However, when we become so holy, so like God, that we see the enormity of sin as He sees it, we shall have no difficulty with the doctrine of eternal punishment.

Expansion: Torrey is like many other Calvinist or Lutheran minded individuals, he wishes to follow the evidence, but instead, desires to call those, who do not find this doctrine Biblical, spiritually blind. I hope that even the most conservative reader can see that as dismissive. Without arguing the evidence, I will say that once again, the truth is biblical, and we must follow it objectively, and not allow theological bias to cloud our judgment. I am recommending that you read, *WHAT IS HELL? Basic Bible Doctrines of the Christian Faith* by Edward D. Andrews[82]

As we look back over the ten classes of difficulties, we see they all arise from our imperfection, and not from the imperfection of the Bible. The Bible is perfect, but we, being imperfect, have difficulty with it. As we grow more and more into the perfection of God, our difficulties grow ever less and less, and so we are forced to conclude that when we become as perfect as God is, we shall have no more difficulties whatever with the Bible.

---

[82] http://www.christianpublishers.org/apps/webstore/products/show/5346167

EDWARD D. ANDREWS

Dealing With Bible Difficulties

By R. A. Torrey

Updated By Edward D. Andrews

Honestly

Whenever you find a difficulty in the Bible frankly, acknowledge it. Do not try to obscure it. Do not try to dodge it. Look it square in the face. Admit it frankly to whoever mentions it. If you cannot give a good, square, honest explanation, do not attempt any at all. Those, who in their zeal for the infallibility of the Bible have attempted explanations of difficulties that do not commend themselves to the honest, fair-minded man, have done untold harm. People have concluded that if these are the best explanations, then there are really no explanations at all, and the Bible instead of being helped has been injured by the unintelligent zeal of foolish friends. If you are not really convinced that the Bible is the Word of God, you can far better afford to wait for an honest solution of a difficulty than you can afford to attempt a solution that is evasive and unsatisfactory.

Humbly

Recognize the limitations of your own mind and knowledge, and do not for a moment imagine that there is no solution just because you have found none. There is, in all probability, a very simple solution, even when you can find no solution at all.

Determinedly

Make up your mind that you will find the solution if you can by any amount of study and hard thinking. The difficulties of the Bible are our heavenly Father's challenge to us to set our brains to work. Do not give up searching for a solution because you cannot find it in five minutes or ten minutes. Ponder over it and work over it for days if necessary. The work will be more beneficial than the solution does. There is a solution somewhere, and you will find it if you will only search for it long enough and hard enough.

Fearlessly

Do not be frightened when you find a difficulty, no matter how unanswerable or how insurmountable it appears at first sight. Thousands of men have encountered just such difficulties, and still, the old Book has withstood the test of time, being the bestseller that will never be touched, in the untold billions of copies. The Bible that has stood eighteen centuries of rigid examination, and of incessant and awful assault, is not likely to go down before your discoveries or before the discharges of any modern critical guns. To one who is at all familiar with the history of critical attacks on the Bible, the confidence of those modern critics who think they are going to annihilate the Bible, at last, is simply amusing.

Patiently

Do not be discouraged because you do not solve every problem in a day. If some difficulty persistently defies your very best efforts at a solution, lay it aside for a while. Later it will likely be resolved, and you will wonder how you were ever perplexed by it.

Scripturally

If you find a difficulty in one part of the Bible, look for another scripture to throw light upon it and dissolve it. Nothing explains scripture like scripture. Repeatedly people have come to me with some difficulty in the Bible that had greatly staggered them and asked for a solution. I have been able to give a solution by simply asking them to read some other chapter and verse, and the simple reading of that scripture has thrown such light upon the passage in question that all the mists have disappeared and the truth has shone as clear as day.

Prayerfully

It is simply wonderful how difficulties dissolve when one looks at them on his knees. Not only does God open our eyes in answer to prayer to behold wonderful things out of His law, but He also opens our eyes to look straight through a difficulty that seemed impenetrable before we prayed. One great reason why many modern Bible scholars have learned to be destructive critics is that they have forgotten how to pray.

EDWARD D. ANDREWS

Bible Difficulties Explained

IT SEEMS THAT the charge that the Bible contradicts itself has been made more and more in the last 20 years. Generally, those making such claims are merely repeating what they have heard because most have not even read the Bible, let alone done an in-depth study of it. I do not wish, however, to set aside all concerns as though they have no merit. There are many who raise legitimate questions that seem, on the surface anyway, to be about well-founded contradiction. Sadly, these issues have caused many to lose their faith in God's Word, the Bible. The purpose of this books is, to help its readers to be able to defend the Bible against Bible critics (1 Pet. 3:15), to contend for the faith (Jude 1:3), and help those, who have begun to doubt. – Jude 1:22-23.

Before we begin explaining things, let us jump right in, getting our feet wet, and deal with two major Bible difficulties, so we can see that there are reasonable, logical answers. After that, we will delve deeper into explaining Bible difficulties.

Is God permitting Human Sacrifice?

Judges 11:29-34, 37-40? Updated American Standard Version (UASV)

29 Then the Spirit of the Lord was upon Jephthah, and he passed through Gilead and Manasseh; and passed on to Mizpah of Gilead, and from Mizpah of Gilead he passed on to the sons of Ammon. 30 And Jephthah **made a vow** to Jehovah and said, "If You will indeed give the sons of Ammon into my hand, 31 then it shall be that **whatever** comes out of the doors of my house to meet me when I return in peace from the sons of Ammon, it shall be Jehovah's, and I will offer it up as a burnt offering." 32 So Jephthah crossed over to the sons of Ammon to fight against them; and Jehovah gave them into his hand. 33 He struck them with a very great slaughter from Aroer as far as Minnith, twenty cities, and as far as Abel-keramim. So the sons of Ammon were subdued before the sons of Israel.

34 When Jephthah came to his house at Mizpah, behold, **his daughter was coming out to meet him** with tambourines and with dancing. Now she was his one and only child; besides her he had no son or daughter.

37 And she said to her father, "Let this thing be done for me: leave me alone two months, that I may go up and down on the mountains and weep because of my virginity, I and my companions." 38 And he said, "Go." So he sent her away for two months; and **she left with her companions, and wept on the mountains because of her virginity.** 39 At the end of two months she returned to her father, who **did to her according to the vow**

that he had made; and she never known a man.[83] Thus it became a custom in Israel, [40] that the daughters of Israel went year by year **to commemorate**[84] **the daughter** of Jephthah the Gileadite four days in the year.

It is true; to infer that having the idea of an animal sacrifice would really have not been an impressive vow, which the context requires. Human sacrifice will be repugnant if we are talking about taking a life. Jephthah had no sons, so he likely knew it was the daughter, who would come to greet him.

First, the text does not say he killed his daughter. The idea of some that he did kill her is concluded only by inference. While it is not good policy to interpret backward, using Paul on Judges, he does say humans are to be **"as a living sacrifice."** Therefore, Jephthah could have offered his daughter at the temple, "as a living sacrifice" in service, like Samuel.

This is not to be taken dismissively, because, under Jewish backgrounds, it is no small thing to offer a **perpetual virginity** as a sacrifice. This would mean Jephthah's lineage would not be carried on, the family name, was no more.

Second, the context says she went out to weep for two months, not mourn her death. It says, "she left with her companions, and **wept on the mountains because of her virginity.**"

If she was facing imminent death, she could have married, and spent that last two months as a married woman. There would be absolutely no reason for her to mourn her virginity if she were not facing perpetual virginity. – Exodus 38:8; 1 Samuel 2:22

Third, it was completely forbidden to offer a human sacrifice. – Leviticus 18:21; 20:2-5; Deuteronomy 12:31; 18:10

Imagine an Israelite believing that he could please God with a human sacrifice that was intended to offer up a human life. To do so would have been a rejection of Jehovah's Sovereignty (the very person you are asking for help), and a rejection of the Law that made them a special people. Worse still, this interpretation would have us believe that Jehovah knew this was coming, allowed the vow, and then aided this type of man to succeed over his enemies.

The last point is simple enough. If such a man as one who would make such a vow, in gross violation of the law, and then carry it out; there is no

---

[83] I.e., *never had relations with a man*
[84] Or *lament*

way he would be mentioned by Paul in Hebrews chapter 11 among the most faithful men and women in Israelite history.

In review, there is no way God would have granted and helped in Jephthah's initial success knowing the vow that was coming because both Jehovah and Jephthah would be as bad as the Canaanites. There is no way that God would accept such a vow and then go on to help Jephthah with his enemies yet again. Then, to allow such a vow to be carried out, to then put Jephthah on the wall of star witnesses for God in Hebrews chapter 11.

Does Isaiah 45:7 mean that God Is the Author of Evil?

Isaiah 45:7 King James Version (KJV) 7 I form the light, and create darkness: I make peace, and **create evil**: I the Lord do all these things.	Isaiah 45:7 English Standard Version (ESV) 7 I form light and create darkness, I make well-being and **create calamity,** I am the Lord, who does all these things.[85]

Encarta Dictionary: (Evil) (1) morally bad: profoundly immoral or wrong (2) deliberately causing great harm, pain, or upset

QUESTION: Is this view of evil always the case? No, as you will see below.

Some apologetic authors try to say, 'we do not understand Isaiah 45:7 correctly, because there are other verses that say God is not evil (1 John 1:5), cannot look approvingly on evil (Hab. 1:13), and cannot be tempted by evil. (James 1:13)' Well, while all of these things are Scripturally true, the question at hand is not: Is God evil, can God approvingly look on evil, or can God be tempted with evil? Those questions are not relevant to the one at hand, as God cannot be those things, and at the same time, he can be the yes to our question. The question is, is God the author, the creator of evil?

We would hardly argue that God was **not** just in his bringing "calamity" or "evil" down on Adam and Eve. Thus, we have Isaiah 45:7 saying that God is the creator of "calamity" or "evil."

Let us begin simple, without trying to be philosophical. When God removed Adam and Eve from the Garden of Eden, he sentenced them and humanity to sickness, old age, and death. (Rom. 5:8; i.e., enforce penalty for sin), which was to bring "calamity" or "evil" upon humankind. Therefore, as we can see "evil" does not always mean wrongdoing. Other examples of God bringing "calamity" or "evil" are Noah and the flood, the Ten Plagues of Egypt, and the destruction of the Canaanites. These acts of

---

[85] See Jeremiah 18:11, Lamentations 3:18, and Amos 3:6

evil were not acts of wrongdoing. Rather, they were righteous and just, because God, the Creator of all things, was administering justice to wrongdoers, to sinners. He warned the perfect first couple what the penalty was for sin. He warned the people for a hundred years by Noah's preaching. He warned the Canaanites centuries before.

Nevertheless, there are times, when God extends mercy, refraining from the execution of his righteous judgment to one worthy of calamity. For example, he warned Nineveh, the city of blood, and they repented, so he pardoned them. (Jonah 3:10) God has made it a practice to warn persons of the results of sin, giving them undeservedly many opportunities to change their ways. – Ezekiel 33:11.

God cannot sin; it is impossible for him to do so. So, when did he create evil? Without getting into the eternity of his knowing what he was going to do, and when, let us just say, evil did not exist when he was the only person in existence. We might say the idea of evil existed because he knew what he was going to do. However, the moment he created creatures (spirit and human), the potential for evil came into existence because both have free will to sin (fall short of perfection). Evil became a reality the moment Satan entertained the idea of causing Adam to sin, to get humanity for himself, and then acted on it.

God has the right and is just to bring the *calamity of* or *evil* down on anyone that is an unrepentant sinner. God did not even have to give us the underserved kindness of offering us his Son. God is the author or agent of evil regardless of the source books that claim otherwise. If he had never created free will beings, evil would have never gone from the idea of evil to the potential of evil, to the existence of evil. However, God felt that it was better to get the sinful state out of angel and human existence, recover, and then any who would sin thereafter; he would be justified in handing out evil or calamity to only that person or angel alone.

Who among us would argue that he should have created humans and angels like robots, automatons with no free will? The moment he chose the free will, he moved evil from an idea to a potential, and Satan moved it to reality. God has a moral nature that does not bring about evil and sin when he is the only person in existence. However, the moment he created beings in his image, which had the potential to sin, he brought about evil. The moment we have a moral code of good and evil that is placed upon one's with free will; then, we have evil as a potential.

In English, the very comprehensive Hebrew word ra' is variously translated as "bad," "downcast (sad, NASB)," "ugly," "evil," "grievous (distressing, NASB)," "sore," "selfish (stingy, HCSB)," and "envious," depending upon the context. (Gen 2:9; 40:7; 41:3; Ex 33:4; Deut. 6:22; 28:35; Pro 23:6; 28:22)

Evil as an adjective **describes** the **quality of** a class of people, places, or things, or of a specific person, place, or thing

Evil as a noun, **defines** the **nature** of a class of people, places, or things, or of a specific person, place, or thing (e.g., the evil one, evil eye).

We can agree that "evil" is a thing. Create means to bring something into existence, be it people, places, or things, as well something abstract, for lack of a better word at the moment. We would agree that when God was alone evil was not a reality; it did not exist? We would agree that the moment that God created free will creatures (angels and humans), creating humans in his image, with his moral nature, he also brought the potential for evil into existence, and it was realized by Satan?

Inerrancy: Can the Bible Be trusted?

If the Bible is the Word of God, it should be in complete agreement throughout; there should be no contradictions. Yet, the rational mind must ask, why is it that some passages appear to be contradictions when compared with others? For example, Numbers 25:9 tells us that 24,000 died from the scourge, whereas at 1 Corinthians 10:8, the apostle Paul says it was 23,000. This would seem to be a clear error. Before addressing such matters, let us first look at some background information.

Full inerrancy in this book means that the original writings are fully without error in all that they state, as are the words. The words were not dictated (automaton), but the intended meaning is inspired, as are the words that convey that meaning. The Author allowed the writer to use his style of writing yet controlled the meaning to the extent of not allowing the writer to choose a wrong word, which would not convey the intended meaning. Other more liberal-minded persons hold with *partial inerrancy*, which claims that as far as faith is concerned, this portion of God's Word is without error, but that there are historical, geographical, and scientific errors.

There are several different levels of inerrancy. *Absolute Inerrancy* is the belief that the Bible is fully true and exact in every way; including not only relationships and doctrine, but also science and history. In other words, all information is completely exact. *Full Inerrancy* is the belief that the Bible was not written as a science or historical textbook, but is phenomenological, in that it is written from the human perspective. In other words, speaking of such things as the sun rising, the four corners of the earth or the rounding off of number approximations are all from a human perspective. *Limited Inerrancy* is the belief that the Bible is meant only as a reflection of God's purposes and will, so the science and history is the understanding of the author's day, and is limited. Thus, the Bible is susceptible to errors in these areas. *Inerrancy of Purpose* is the belief that it is only inerrant in the purpose of bringing its readers to a saving faith. The Bible is not about facts, but about persons and relationships, thus, it is subject to error. *Inspired: Not Inerrant* is the belief that its authors are human and thus subject to human error. It should be noted that this author holds the position of full inerrancy.

For many today, the Bible is nothing more than a book written by men. The Bible critic believes the Bible to be full of myths and legends, contradictions, and geographical, historical, and scientific errors. University professor Gerald A. Larue had this to say, "The views of the writers as expressed in the Bible reflect the ideas, beliefs, and concepts current in their own times and are limited by the extent of knowledge in those times."[86] On the other hand, the Bible's authors claim that their writings were inspired of God, as Holy Spirit moved them along. We will discover shortly that the Bible critics have much to say, but it is inflated or empty.

2 Timothy 3:16-17 Updated American Standard Version (UASV)

[16] All Scripture is inspired by God and profitable for teaching, for reproof, for correction, for training in righteousness; [17] so that the man of God may be fully competent, equipped for every good work.

2 Peter 1:21 Updated American Standard Version (UASV)

[21] for no prophecy was ever produced by the will of man, but men carried along by the Holy Spirit spoke from God.

The question remains as to whether the Bible is a book written by imperfect men and full of errors, or is written by imperfect men, but inspired by God. If the Bible is just another book by imperfect man, there is no hope for humankind. If it is inspired by God and without error, although penned by imperfect men, we have the hope of everything that it offers: a rich, happy life now by applying counsel that lies within and the real life that is to come, everlasting life. This author contends that the Bible is inspired of God and free of human error, although written by imperfect humans.

Before we take on the critics who seem to sift the Scriptures looking for problematic verses, let us take a moment to reflect on how we should approach these alleged problem texts. The critic's argument goes something like this: 'If God does not err and the Bible is the Word of God, then the Bible should not have one single error or contradiction, yet it is full of errors

---

[86] Gerald Larue, "The Bible as a Political Weapon," *Free Inquiry* (Summer 1983): 39.

and contradictions.' If the Bible is riddled with nothing but contradictions and errors as the critics would have us believe, why, out of 31,173 verses in the Bible, should there be only 2-3 thousand Bible difficulties that are called into question, this being less than ten percent of the whole?

First, let it be said that it is every Christian's obligation to get a deeper understanding of God's Word, just as the apostle Paul told Timothy:

1 Timothy 4:15-16 Updated American Standard Version (UASV)

[15] Practice these things, be absorbed in them, so that your progress will be evident to all. [16] Pay close attention to yourself and to your teaching; persevere in these things, for as you do this you will ensure salvation both for yourself and for those who hear you.

Paul also told the Corinthians:

2 Corinthians 10:4-5 Updated American Standard Version (UASV)

[4] For the weapons of our warfare are not of the flesh[87] but powerful to God for destroying strongholds.[88] [5] We are destroying speculations and every lofty thing raised up against the knowledge of God, and we are taking every thought captive to the obedience of Christ,

Paul also told the Philippians:

Philippians 1:7 Updated American Standard Version (UASV)

[7] It is right for me to feel thus about you all, because I hold you in my heart, for you are all partakers with me of grace, both in my imprisonment and in the defense and confirmation of the gospel.

In being able to defend against the modern-day critic, one has to be able to reason from the Scriptures and overturn the critic's argument(s) with mildness. If someone were to approach us about an alleged error or contradiction, what should we do? We should be frank and honest. If we do not have an answer, we should admit such. If the text in question gives the appearance of difficulty, we should admit this as well. If we are unsure as to how we should answer, we can simply say that we will look into it and get back to them, returning with a reasonable answer.

However, we do not want to express disbelief and doubt to our critics, because they will be emboldened in their disbelief. It will put them on the offense and us on the defense. With great confidence, we can express that there is an answer. The Bible has withstood the test of 2,000 years of persecution and interrogation and yet it is the most printed book of all

---

[87] That is *merely human*
[88] That is *tearing down false arguments*

time, currently being translated into 2,287 languages. If these critical questions were so threatening, the Bible would not be the book that it is.

When we are pursuing the text in question, be unwavering in purpose, or resolved to find an answer. In some cases, it may take hours of digging to find the solution. Consider this: as we resolve these difficulties, we are also building our faith that God's Word is inerrant. Moreover, we will want to do preventative maintenance in our personal study. As we are doing our Bible reading, take note of these surface discrepancies and resolve them as we work our way through the Bible. We need to make this part of our prayers as well. I recommend the following program. Below are several books that deal with difficult passages. As we daily read and study our Bible from Genesis to Revelation, do not attempt it in one year; make it a four-year program. Use a good exegetical commentary like *The Holman Old/New Testament Commentary* (HOTC/HNTC) or *The New American Commentary* set, and *The Big Book of Bible Difficulties* by Norman L. Geisler, as well as *The Encyclopedia of Bible Difficulties* by Gleason Archer.

We should be aware that men under inspiration penned the originally written books. In fact, we do not have those originals, what textual scholars call autographs, but we do have thousands of copies. The copyists, however, were not inspired; therefore, as one might expect, throughout the first 1,400 years of copying, thousands of errors were transmitted into the texts that were being copied by imperfect hands that were not under inspiration when copying. Yet, the next 450 years saw a restoration of the text by textual scholars from around the world. Therefore, while many of our best literal translations today may not be inspired, they are a mirror-like reflection of the autographs by way of textual criticism.[89] Therefore, the fallacy could be with the copyist error that has simply not been weeded out. In addition, we must keep in mind that God's Word is without error, but our interpretation and understanding of that Word is not.

It should be noted that the Bible is made up of 66 smaller books that were hand-written over a period of 1,600 years, having some 40 writers of various trades such as shepherd, king, priest, tax collector, governor, physician, copyist, fisherman, and a tentmaker. Therefore, it should not surprise us that some difficulties are encountered as we casually read the Bible. Yet, if one were to take a deeper look, one would find that these difficulties are easily explained. Let us take a few pages to examine some passages that have been under attack.

---

[89] Textual criticism is the study of copies of any written work of which the autograph (original) is unknown, with the purpose of ascertaining the original text. Harold J. Green, Introduction to New Testament Textual Criticism (Peabody, MA: Hendrickson, 1995), 1.

This chapter's objective is not to be exhaustive, not even close. What we are looking to do is cover a few alleged contradictions and a couple of alleged mistakes. This is to give us a small sampling of the reasonable answers that we will find in the above recommended books. Remember, our Bible is a sword that we must use both offensively and defensively. One must wonder how long a warrior of ancient times would last who was not expertly trained in the use of his weapon. Let us look at a few scriptures that support our need to learn our Bible well so will be able to defend what we believe to be true.

When "false apostles, deceitful workmen, disguising themselves as apostles of Christ" were causing trouble in the congregation in Corinth, the apostle Paul wrote that under such circumstances, we are to *tear down their arguments* and *take every thought captive*. (2 Corinthians 10:4, 5; 11:13–15) All who present critical arguments against God's Word, or contrary to it, can have their arguments overturned by the Christian, who is able and ready to defend that Word in mildness. – 2 Timothy 2:24–26.

1 Peter 3:15 Updated American Standard Version (UASV)

[15] but sanctify Christ as Lord in your hearts, always being prepared to make a defense[90] to anyone who asks you for a reason for the hope that is in you; yet do it with gentleness and respect;

Peter says that we need to be prepared to make a *defense*. The Greek word behind the English 'defense' is *apologia*, which is actually a legal term that refers to the defense of a defendant in court. Our English apologetics is just what Peter spoke of, having the ability to give a reason to any who may challenge us, or to answer those who are not challenging us but who have honest questions that deserve to be answered.

2 Timothy 2:24-25 Updated American Standard Version (UASV)

[24] For a slave of the Lord does not need to fight, but needs to be kind to all, qualified to teach, showing restraint when wronged [25] with gentleness correcting those who are in opposition, if perhaps God may grant them repentance leading to accurate knowledge[91] of the truth,

Look at the Greek word (*epignosis*) behind the English "knowledge" in the above. "It is more intensive than *gnosis* (1108), knowledge because it expresses a more thorough participation in the acquiring of knowledge on the part of the learner."[92] The requirement of all of the Lord's servants

---

[90] Or *argument*, or *explanation*

[91] *Epignosis* is a strengthened or intensified form of *gnosis* (*epi*, meaning "additional"), meaning, "true," "real," "full," "complete" or "accurate," depending upon the context. Paul and Peter alone use *epignosis*.

[92] Spiros Zodhiates, *The Complete Word Study Dictionary: New Testament*, Electronic ed. (Chattanooga, TN: AMG Publishers, 2000, c1992, c1993), S. G1922.

is that they be able to teach, but not in a quarrelsome way, and in a way to correct his opponents with mildness. Why? Because the purpose of it all is that by God, and through the Christian teacher, one may come to repentance and begin taking in an accurate knowledge of the truth.

Inerrancy: Practical Principles to Overcoming Bible Difficulties

Below are several ways of looking at the Bible that enable the reader to see he is not dealing with an error or contradiction, but rather a Bible difficulty.

Different Points of View

At times, you may have two different writers who are writing from two different points of view.

Numbers 35:14 Updated American Standard Version (UASV)

[14] You shall give three cities across the Jordan and three cities you shall give in the land of Canaan; they will be cities of refuge.

Joshua 22:4 Updated American Standard Version (UASV)

[4] And now Jehovah your God has given rest to your brothers, as he spoke to them; therefore turn now and go to your tents, to the land of your possession, which Moses the servant of Jehovah gave you beyond the Jordan. [on the other side of the Jordan, ESV]

Here we see that Moses is speaking about the east side of the Jordan when he says "on this side of the Jordan." Joshua, on the other hand, is also speaking about the east side of the Jordan when he says "on the other side of the Jordan." So, who is correct? Both are. When Moses was penning Numbers the Israelites had not yet crossed the Jordan River, so the east side was "this side," the side he was on. On the other hand, when Joshua penned his book, the Israelites had crossed the Jordan, so the east side was just as he had said, "on the other side of the Jordan." Thus, we should not assume that two different writers are writing from the same perspective.

A Careful Reading

At times, it may simply be a case of needing to slow down and carefully read the account, considering exactly what is being said.

Joshua 18:28 Updated American Standard Version (UASV)

²⁸ and Zelah, Haeleph and the Jebusite (that is, Jerusalem), Gibeah, Kiriath; fourteen cities with their villages. This is the inheritance of the sons of Benjamin according to their families.

Judges 1:21 Updated American Standard Version (UASV)

²¹ But the sons of Benjamin did not drive out the Jebusites who lived in Jerusalem; so the Jebusites have lived with the sons of Benjamin in Jerusalem to this day.

Joshua 15:63 Updated American Standard Version (UASV)

⁶³ But as for the Jebusites, the inhabitants of Jerusalem, the sons of Judah could not drive them out; so the Jebusites live with the sons of Judah at Jerusalem until this day.

Judges 1:8-9 Updated American Standard Version (UASV)

⁸ And then the sons of Judah fought against Jerusalem and captured it and struck it with the edge of the sword and set the city on fire. ⁹ And afterward the sons of Judah went down to fight against the Canaanites living in the hill country and in the Negev[93] and in the Shephelah.[94]

2 Samuel 5:5-9 Updated American Standard Version (UASV)

⁵ At Hebron he reigned over Judah seven years and six months, and in Jerusalem he reigned thirty-three years over all Israel and Judah.

⁶ And the king and his men went to Jerusalem against the Jebusites, the inhabitants of the land, and they said to David, "You shall not come in here, but the blind and lame will turn you away"; thinking, "David cannot come in here." ⁷ Nevertheless, David captured the stronghold of Zion, that is the city of David. ⁸ And David said on that day, "Whoever would strike the Jebusites, let him get up the water shaft to attack 'the lame and the blind,' who are hated by David's soul." Therefore it is said, "The blind and the lame shall not come into the house." ⁹ And David lived in the stronghold and called it the city of David. And David built all around from the Millo and inward.

There is no doubt that even the advanced Bible reader of many years can come away confused because the above accounts seem to be contradictory. In Joshua 18:28 and Judges 1:21, we see that Jerusalem was an inheritance of the tribe of Benjamin, yet the Benjamites were unable to conquer Jerusalem. However, in Joshua 15:63 we see that the tribe of Judah could not conquer them either, with the reading giving the impression that it was a part of their inheritance. In Judges 1:8, however, Judah was eventually able to conquer Jerusalem and burn it with fire. Yet,

---

⁹³ I.e. *South*
⁹⁴ I.e., lowland

to add even more to the confusion, we find at 2 Samuel 5:5–8 that David is said to have conquered Jerusalem hundreds of years later.

Now that we have the particulars let us look at it more clearly. The boundary between Benjamin's inheritances ran right through the middle of Jerusalem. Joshua 8:28 is correct, in that what would later be called the "city of David" was in the territory of Benjamin, but it also in part crossed over the line into the territory of Judah, causing both tribes to go to war against this Jebusite city. It is also true that the tribe of Benjamin was unable to conquer the city and that the tribe of Judah eventually did. However, if you look at Judges 1:9 again, you will see that Judah did not finish the job entirely and moved on to conquer other areas. This allowed the remaining ones to regroup and form a resistance that neither Benjamin nor Judah could overcome, so these Jebusites remained until the time of David, hundreds of years later.

Intended Meaning of Writer

First, the Bible student needs to understand the level that the Bible intends to be exact in what is written. If Jim told a friend that 650 graduated with him from high school in 1984, it is not challenged, because it is all too clear that he is using rounded numbers and is not meaning to be exactly precise. This is how God's Word operates as well. Sometimes it means to be exact, at other times, it is simply rounding numbers, in other cases, the intention of the writer is a general reference, to give readers of that time and succeeding generations some perspective. Did Samuel, the author of Judges, intend to pen a book on the chronology of Judges, or was his focus on the falling away, oppression, and the rescue by a judge, repeatedly. Now, it would seem that Jeremiah, the author of 1 Kings was more interested in giving his readers an exact number of years.

Acts 2:41 Updated American Standard Version (UASV)

[41] So those who received his word were baptized, and there were added that day about three thousand souls.

As you can see here, numbers within the Bible are often used with approximations. This is a frequent practice even today, in both written works and verbal conversation.

Acts 7:2-3 Updated American Standard Version (UASV)

[2] And Stephen said:

"Brothers and fathers, hear me. The God of glory appeared to our father Abraham when he was in Mesopotamia, before he lived in

Haran, ³ and said to him, 'Go out from your land and from your kindred and go into the land that I will show you.'

If you were to check the Hebrew Scriptures at Genesis 12:1, you would find that what is claimed to have been said by God to Abraham is not quoted word-for-word; it is simply a paraphrase. This is a normal practice within Scripture and in writing in general.

Numbers 34:15 Updated American Standard Version (UASV)

¹⁵ The two and a half tribes have received their inheritance beyond the Jordan opposite Jericho, eastward toward the sunrising."

Just as you would read in today's local newspaper, the Bible writer has written from the human standpoint, how it appeared to him. The Bible also speaks of "to the end of the earth" (Psalm 46:9), "from the four corners of the earth" (Isa 11:12), and "the four winds of the earth" (Revelation 7:1). These phrases are still used today.

Unexplained Does Not mean Unexplainable

Considering that there are 31,173 verses in the Bible, encompassing 66 books written by about 40 writers, ranging from shepherds to kings, an army general, fishermen, tax collector, a physician and on and on, and being penned over a 1,600 year period, one does find a few hundred Bible difficulties (about one percent). However, 99 percent of those are explainable. Yet no one wants to be so arrogant to say that he can explain them all. It has nothing to do with the inadequacy of God's Word but is based on human understanding. In many cases, science or archaeology and the field of custom and culture of ancient peoples has helped explain difficulties in hundreds of passages. Therefore, there may be less than one percent left to be answered, yet our knowledge of God's Word continues to grow.

Guilty Until Proven Innocent

This is exactly the perception that the critic has of God's Word. The legal principle of being "innocent until proven guilty" afforded mankind in courts of justice is withheld from the very Word of God. What is ironic here is that this policy has contributed to these Bible critics looking foolish over and over again when something comes to light that vindicates the portion of Scripture they are challenging.

Daniel 5:1 Updated American Standard Version (UASV)

¹ Belshazzar the king made⁹⁵ a great feast for a thousand of his nobles, and he was drinking wine in the presence of the thousand.

Bible critics had long claimed that Belshazzar was not known outside of the book Daniel; therefore, they argue that Daniel was mistaken. Yet it hardly seems prudent to argue error from absence of outside evidence. Just because archaeology had not discovered such a person did not mean that Daniel was wrong, or that such a person did not exist. In 1854, some small clay cylinders were discovered in modern-day southern Iraq, which would have been the city of Ur in ancient Babylonia. The cuneiform documents were a prayer of King Nabonidus for "Bel-sar-ussur, my eldest son." These tablets also showed that this "Bel-sar-ussur" had secretaries as well as a household staff. Other tablets were discovered a short time later that showed that the kingship was entrusted to this eldest son as a coregent while his father was away.

He entrusted the 'Camp' to his oldest (son), the firstborn [Belshazzar], the troops everywhere in the country he ordered under his (command). He let (everything) go, entrusted the kingship to him and, himself, he [Nabonidus] started out for a long journey, the (military) forces of Akkad marching with him; he turned towards Tema (deep) in the west."⁹⁶

Ignoring Literary Styles

The Bible is a diverse book when it comes to literary styles: narrative, poetic, prophetic, and apocalyptic; also containing parables, metaphors, similes, hyperbole, and other figures of speech. Too often, these alleged errors are the result of a reader taking a figure of speech as literal, or reading a parable as though it is a narrative.

Matthew 24:35 Updated American Standard Version (UASV)

³⁵ Heaven and earth will pass away, but my words will not pass away.

If some do not recognize that they are dealing with a figure of speech, they are bound to come away with the wrong meaning. Some have concluded from Matthew 24:35 that Jesus was speaking of an eventual destruction of the earth. This is hardly the case, as his listeners would not have understood it that way based on their understanding of the Old Testament. They would have understood that he was simply being emphatic about the words he spoke, using hyperbole. What he was conveying is that his words are more enduring than heaven and earth, and

---

⁹⁵ I.e., held
⁹⁶ J. Pritchard, ed., *Ancient Near Eastern Texts* (1974), 313.

with heaven and earth being understood as eternal, this merely conveyed even more so that Jesus' words could be trusted.

Two Accounts of the Same Incident

If you were to speak to officers that take accident reports for their police department, you would find that there is cohesion in the accounts, but each person has merely witnessed aspects that have stood out to them. We will see that this is the case as well with the examples below, which is the same account in two different gospels:

Matthew 8:5 Updated American Standard Version (UASV)

[5] When he[97] had entered Capernaum, a centurion came forward to him, imploring him,

Luke 7:2-3 Updated American Standard Version (UASV)

[2] And a centurion's[98] slave, who was highly regarded[99] by him, was sick and about to die. [3] When he heard about Jesus, he sent some older men of the Jews[100] asking him to come and bring his slave safely through.[101]

Immediately we see the problem of whether the centurion or the elders of the Jews spoke with Jesus. The solution is not really hidden from us. Which of the two accounts is the most detailed account? You are correct if you said, Luke. The centurion sent the elders of the Jews to represent him to Jesus, so; that whatever response Jesus might give, it would be as though he were addressing the centurion; therefore, Matthew gave his readers the basic thought, not seeing the need of mentioning the elders of the Jews aspect. This is how a representative was viewed in the first century, just as some countries see ambassadors today as being the very person they represent. Therefore, both Matthew and Luke are correct.

Man's Fallible Interpretations

Inspiration by God is infallible, without error. Imperfect man and his interpretations over the centuries, as bad as many of them have been, should not cast a shadow over God's inspired Word. The entire Word of God has one meaning and one meaning only for every penned word, which is what God willed to be conveyed by the human writer he chose to use.

---

[97] That is *Jesus*
[98] I.e., army officer over a hundred solderiers
[99] Lit *to whom he was honorable*
[100] Or *Jewish elders*
[101] I.e., *save the life of his slave*

The Autograph Alone Is Inspired and Inerrant

It has been argued by conservative scholars that only the autograph manuscripts were inspired and inerrant, not the copying of those manuscripts over the next 3,000 years for the Old Testament and 1,500 years for the New Testament. While I would agree with this position as well, it should be noted that we do not possess the autographs, so to argue that they are inerrant is to speak of nonexistent documents. However, it should be further understood that through the science of textual criticism, we can establish a mirror reflection of the autograph manuscripts. B. F. Westcott, F. J. A. Hort, F. F. Bruce, and many other textual scholars would agree with Norman L Geisler's assessment: "The New Testament, then, has not only survived in more manuscripts than any other book from antiquity, but it has survived in a purer form than any other great book—*a form that is 99.5 percent pure.*"[102]

An example of a copyist error can be found in Luke's genealogy of Jesus at Luke 3:35–37. In verse 37 you will find a Cainan, and in verse 36 you will find a second Cainan between Arphaxad (Arpachshad) and Shelah. As one can see from most footnotes in different study Bibles, the Cainan in verse 36 is seen as a scribal error, and is not found in the Hebrew Old Testament, the Samaritan Pentateuch, or the Aramaic Targums, but is found in the Greek Septuagint. (Genesis 10:24; 11:12, 13; 1 Chronicles 1:18, but not 1 Chronicles 1:24) It seems quite unlikely that it was in the earlier copies of the Septuagint, because the first-century Jewish historian Josephus lists Shelah next as the son of Arphaxad, and Josephus normally followed the Septuagint.[103] So one might ask why this second Cainan is found in the translations at all if this is the case? The manuscripts that do contain this second Cainan are some of the best manuscripts that are used in establishing the original text: 01 B L A¹ 33 (Kainam); A 038 044 0102 A¹³ (Kainan).

Look at the Context

Many alleged inconsistencies disappear by simply looking at the context. Taking words out of context can distort their meaning. *Merriam-Webster's Collegiate Dictionary* defines context as "the parts of a discourse that surround a word or passage and can throw light on its meaning."[104] Context can also be "the circumstances or events that form the environment within which something exists or takes place." If we were to look in a thesaurus for a synonym, we would find "background" for this second meaning. At 2 Timothy 2:15, the apostle Paul brings home the point of why

---

[102] Norman L. Geisler and William E. Nix: *A General Introduction to the Bible* (Chicago, Moody Press, 1980), 367. (Emphasis is mine.)

[103] *Jewish Antiquities,* I, 146 [vi, 4].

[104] Merriam-Webster, Inc: *Merriam-Webster's Collegiate Dictionary.* Eleventh ed. (Springfield, Mass.: Merriam-Webster, Inc. 2003).

context is so important: "Do your best to present yourself to God as one approved, a worker who has no need to be ashamed, rightly handling the word of truth."

Ephesians 2:8-9 Updated American Standard Version (UASV)

[8] For by grace you have been saved through faith; and that not of yourselves, it is the gift of God; [9] not from works, so that no man may boast.

James 2:26 Updated American Standard Version (UASV)

[26] For as the body apart from the spirit[105] is dead, so also faith apart from works is dead.

So, which is it? Is salvation possible by faith alone as Paul wrote to the Ephesians, or is faith dead without works as James wrote to his readers? As our subtitle brings out, let us look at the context. In the letter to the Ephesians, the apostle Paul is speaking to the Jewish Christians who were looking to the works of the Mosaic Law as a means to salvation, a righteous standing before God. Paul was telling these legalistic Jewish Christians that this is not so. In fact, this would invalidate Christ's ransom because there would have been no need for it if one could achieve salvation by meticulously keeping the Mosaic Law. (Rom. 5:18) But James was writing to those in a congregation who were concerned with their status before other men, who were looking for prominent positions within the congregation, and not taking care of those that were in need. (Jam. 2:14–17) So, James is merely addressing those who call themselves Christian, but in name only. No person could truly be a Christian and not possess some good works, such as feeding the poor, helping the elderly. This type of work was an evident demonstration of one's Christian personality. Paul was in perfect harmony with James on this. – Romans 10:10; 1 Corinthians 15:58; Ephesians 5:15, 21–33; 6:15; 1 Timothy 4:16; 2 Timothy 4:5; Hebrews 10:23-25.

Inerrancy: Are There Contradictions?

Below I will follow this pattern. I will list the critic's argument first, followed by the text of difficulty, and conclude with an answer to the critic. What should be kept at the forefront of our mind is this: one is simply looking for the best answer, not absoluteness. If there is a reasonable answer to a Bible difficulty, why are the critics able to set them aside with ease? Because they start with the premise that this is not the Word of God, but only a book by imperfect men and full of contradictions; thus, the bias toward errors has blinded their judgment.

---

[105] Or *breath*

Critic: The critic would argue that there was an Adam and Eve, and an Abel who was now dead, so, where did Cain get his wife? This is one of the most common questions by Bible critics.

Genesis 4:17 Updated American Standard Version (UASV)

[17] Cain had sexual relations[106] with his wife and she conceived, and gave birth to Enoch; and he built a city, and called the name of the city Enoch, after the name of his son, Enoch.

Answer: If one were to read a little further along, they would come to the realization that Adam had a son named Seth; it further adds that Adam "became father to sons *and daughters.*" (Genesis 5:4) Adam lived for a total of 800 years after fathering Seth, giving him ample opportunity to father many more sons and daughters. So it could be that Cain married one of his sisters. If he waited until one of his brothers and sisters had a daughter, he could have married one of his nieces once she was old enough. In the beginning, humans were closer to perfection; this explains why they lived longer and why at that time there was little health risk of genetic defects in the case of children born to closely related parents, in contrast to how it is today. As time passed, genetic defects increased and life spans decreased. Adam lived to see 930 years. Yet Shem, who lived after the Flood, died at 600 years, while Shem's son Arpachshad only lived 438 years, dying before his father died. Abraham saw an even greater decrease in that he only lived 175 years while his grandson Jacob was 147 years when he died. Thus, due to increasing imperfection, God prohibited the marriage of closely related people under the Mosaic Law because of the likelihood of genetic defects.—Leviticus 18:9.

Critic: If God is here hardening Pharaoh's heart, what exactly makes Pharaoh responsible for the decisions he makes?

Exodus 4:21 Updated American Standard Version (UASV)

[21] Jehovah said to Moses, "When you go and return to Egypt see that you perform before Pharaoh all the wonders which I have put in your hand; but I will harden his heart so that he will not let the people go.

Answer: This is actually a prophecy. God knew that what he was about to do would contribute to a stubborn and obstinate Pharaoh, who was going to be unwilling to change or give up the Israelites so they could go off to worship their God. Therefore, this is not stating what God is going to do; it is prophesying that Pharaoh's heart will harden because of the actions of God. The fact is, Pharaoh allowed his own heart to harden because he was determined not to agree with Moses' wishes or accept

---

[106] Lit *knew*

Jehovah's request to let the people go. Moses tells us at Exodus 7:13 (ESV) that "Pharaoh's heart was hardened, and he would not listen to them, as the Lord had said." Again, at 8:15 we read, "When Pharaoh saw that there was a respite, he hardened his heart and would not listen to them, as the Lord had said."

Critic: The Israelites had just received the Ten Commandments, with one commandment being: "You shall not make for yourself a carved image or any likeness of anything that is in heaven above, or that is in the earth beneath, or that is in the water under the earth." Therefore, how is the bronze serpent not a violation of this commandment?

Numbers 21:9 Updated American Standard Version (UASV)

9 And Moses made a bronze serpent and set it on the standard;[107] and it came about, that if a serpent bit any man, when he looked to the bronze serpent, he lived.

Answer: First, an idol is "a representation or symbol of an object of worship; *broadly*: a false god."[108] Second, it should be noted that not all images are idols. The bronze serpent was not made for the purpose of worship, or for some passionate devotion or veneration. There were times, however, when images were created with absolutely no intention of it receiving devotion, veneration, or worship, yet were later made into objects of veneration. That is exactly what happened with the copper serpent that Moses had formed in the wilderness. Many centuries later, "in the third year of Hoshea son of Elah, king of Israel, Hezekiah the son of Ahaz, king of Judah, began to reign. He removed the high places and broke the pillars and cut down the Asherah. And he broke in pieces the bronze serpent that Moses had made; for until those days the people of Israel had made offerings to it (it was called Nehushtan)."—2 Kings 18:1, 4.

Critic: Deuteronomy 15:11 (NET) says: "*There will never cease to be some poor people in the land;* therefore, I am commanding you to make sure you open your hand to your fellow Israelites who are needy and poor in your land." Is this not a contradiction of Deuteronomy 15:4? Will there be no poor among the Israelites, or will there be poor among them? Which is it?

Deuteronomy 15:4 Updated American Standard Version (UASV)

4 However, there will be no poor among you, since Jehovah will surely bless you in the land which Jehovah your God is giving you as an inheritance to possess,

---

107 I.e., *pole*
108 Merriam-Webster, Inc: *Merriam-Webster's Collegiate Dictionary.* Eleventh ed. (Springfield, Mass.: Merriam-Webster, Inc., 2003).

Answer: If you look at the context, Deuteronomy 15:4 is stating that if the Israelites obey Jehovah's command to take care of the poor, "there should not be any poor among" them. Thus, for every poor person, there will be one to take care of that need. If an Israelite fell on hard times, there was to be a fellow Israelite ready to step in to help him through those hard times. Verse 11 stresses the truth of the imperfect world since the rebellion of Adam and inherited sin: there will always be poor among mankind, the Israelites being no different. However, the difference with God's people is that those who were well off financially were to offset conditions for those who fell on difficult times. This is not to be confused with the socialistic welfare systems in the world today. Those Jews were hard-working men, who labored from sunup to sundown to take care of their families. But if disease overtook their herd or unseasonal weather brought about failed crops, an Israelite could sell himself into the service of a fellow Israelite for a period of time; thereafter, he would be back on his feet. And many years down the road, he may very well do the same for another Israelite, who fell on difficult times.

Critic: Joshua 11:23 says that Joshua took the land according to what God had spoken to Moses and handed it on to the nation of Israel as planned. However, in Joshua 13:1, God is telling Joshua that he has grown old and much of the Promised Land has yet to be taken possession of. How can both be true? Is this not a contradiction?

Joshua 11:23 Updated American Standard Version (UASV)

²³ So Joshua took the whole land, according to all that Jehovah had spoken to Moses, and Joshua gave it for an inheritance to Israel according to their divisions by their tribes, and the land had rest from war.

Joshua 13:1 Updated American Standard Version (UASV)

13 Now Joshua was old and advanced in years, and Jehovah said to him, "You are old and advanced in years, and there remains yet very much land to possess.

Answer: No, it is not a contradiction. When the Israelites were to take the land, it was to take place in two different stages: the nation as a whole was to go to war and defeat the 31 kings of this land; thereafter, each Israelite tribe was to take their part of the land based on their individual actions. (Joshua 17:14–18; 18:3) Joshua fulfilled his role, which is expressed in 11:23 while the individual tribes did not complete their campaigns, which is expressed in 13:1. Even though the individual tribes failed to live up to taking their portion, the remaining Canaanites posed no real threat. Joshua 21:44, *ASV*, reads: "Jehovah gave them rest round about."

Critic: The critic would point out that John 1:18 clearly says that "*no one has ever seen God,*" while Exodus 24:10 explicitly states that Moses and Aaron, Nadab and Abihu, and seventy of the elders of Israel "*saw the God of Israel.*" Worse still, God informs them in Exodus 33:20: "You cannot see my face, for man shall not see me and live." The critic with his knowing smile says, 'This is a blatant contradiction.'

John 1:18 Updated American Standard Version (UASV)

18 No one has seen God at any time; the only begotten god[109] who is in the bosom of the Father,[110] that one has made him fully known.

Exodus 24:10 Updated American Standard Version (UASV)

10 and they saw the God of Israel; and under his feet was what seemed like a sapphire pavement, as clear as the sky itself.

Exodus 33:20 Updated American Standard Version (UASV)

20 But he [God] said, "You cannot see my face, for no man can see me and live!"

Answer: Exodus 33:20 is one-hundred percent correct: No human could see Jehovah God and live. The apostle Paul at Colossians 1:15 tell us that Christ is the image of the invisible God, and the writer informs us at Hebrews 1:3 that Jesus is the "exact representation of His nature." Yet if you were to read the account of Saul of Tarsus (the apostle Paul), you would see that a mere partial manifestation of Christ's glory blinded Saul – Acts 9:1–18.

When the Bible says that Moses and others have seen God, it is not speaking of *literally* seeing him, because first of all He is an invisible spirit person. It is a *manifestation* of his glory, which is an act of showing or demonstrating his presence, making himself perceptible to the human mind. In fact, it is generally an angelic representative that stands in his place and not him personally. Exodus 24:16 informs us that "the glory of the Lord dwelt on Mount Sinai," not the Lord himself personally. When texts such as Exodus 24:10 explicitly state that Moses and Aaron, Nadab and Abihu, and seventy of the elders of Israel "*saw the God of Israel,*" it is this "glory of the Lord," an angelic representative. This is shown to be the case at Luke 2:9, which reads: "And *an angel of the Lord* appeared to them, and *the glory of the Lord shone around them* [the shepherds], and they were filled with fear."

Many Bible difficulties are cleared up elsewhere in Scripture; for example, in the New Testament, you will find a text clarifying a difficulty

---

109 Jn 1:18: "only-begotten god", P66א*BC*Lsyrhmg.p; **[V1]** "the only-begotten god," P75133אcopbo; **[V2]** "the only-begotten Son." AC3(Ws)QYfl.13 MajVgSyrc
110 Or *at the Father's side*

from the Old Testament, such as Acts 7:53, which refers to those "who received the law *as delivered by angels* and did not keep it." Support comes from Paul at Galatians 3:19: "Why then the law? It was added because of transgressions until the offspring should come to whom the promise had been made, and it was put in place through angels by an intermediary." The writer of Hebrews chimes in at 2:2 with "For since the message *declared by angels* proved to be reliable, and every transgression or disobedience received a just retribution. . . ." As we travel back to Exodus again, to 19:19 specifically, we find support that it was not God's own voice, which Moses heard; no, it was an angelic representative, for it reads: "Moses was speaking, and God was answering him with a voice." Exodus 33:22–23 also helps us to appreciate that it was the back of these angelic representatives of Jehovah that Moses saw: "While my glory passes by . . . Then I will take away my hand, and you shall see my back, but my face shall not be seen."

Exodus 3:4 states: "God called to him out of the bush, 'Moses, Moses!' And he said, 'Here I am.'" Verse 6 informs us: "I am the God of your father, the God of Abraham, the God of Isaac, and the God of Jacob." Yet, in verse 2 we read: "And the angel of the Lord appeared to him in a flame of fire out of the midst of a bush." Here is another example of using God's Word to clear up what seems to be unclear or difficult to understand at first glance. Thus, while it speaks of the Lord making a direct appearance, it is really an angelic representative. Even today, we hear such comments, as 'the president of the United States is to visit the Middle East later this week.' However, later in the article it is made clear that he is not going personally, but it is one of his high-ranking representatives. Let us close with two examples, starting with,

Genesis 32:24-30 Updated American Standard Version (UASV)

²⁴ And Jacob was left alone, and a man wrestled with him until daybreak. ²⁵ When he saw that he had not prevailed against him, he touched the socket of his thigh; so the socket of Jacob's thigh was dislocated as he wrestled with him. ²⁶ Then he said, "Let me go, for the dawn is breaking." But he said, "I will not let you go unless you bless me." ²⁷ And he said to him, "What is your name?" And he said, "Jacob." ²⁸ And he said, "Your name shall no longer be called Jacob, but Israel,¹¹¹ for you have struggled with God and with men and have prevailed." ²⁹ Then Jacob asked him and said, "Please tell me your name." But he said, "Why is it that you ask my name?" And he blessed him there. ³⁰ So Jacob named the place

---
¹¹¹ Meaning *he contends with God*

Peniel,[112] for he said, "I have seen God face to face, yet my soul has been preserved."

It is all too obvious here that this man is simply a materialized angel in the form of a man, another angelic representative of Jehovah God. Moreover, the reader of this book should have taken in that the Israelites as a whole saw these angelic representatives and spoke of them as though they were dealing directly with Jehovah God himself.

This proved to be the case in the second example found in the book of Judges where an angelic representative visited Manoah and his wife. Like the above mentioned account, Manoah and his wife treated this angelic representative as if he were Jehovah God himself: "And Manoah said to the angel of the Lord, 'What is your name, so that, when your words come true, we may honor you?' And the angel of the Lord said to him, 'Why do you ask my name, seeing it is wonderful?' Then Manoah knew that he was the angel of the Lord. And Manoah said to his wife, "We shall surely die, *for we have seen God*." – Judges 13:3–22.

Inerrancy: Are There Mistakes?

I have addressed the alleged contradictions, so it would seem that our job is done here, right? Not hardly. Yes, there are just as many who claim that the Bible is full of mistakes.

Critic: Matthew 27:5 states that Judas hanged himself, whereas Acts 1:18 says, "Falling headlong, he burst open in the middle and all his intestines gushed out."

Matthew 27:5 Updated American Standard Version (UASV)

[5] And he threw the pieces of silver into the temple and departed; and he went away and hanged himself.

Acts 1:18 Updated American Standard Version (UASV)

[18] (Now this man acquired a field with the price of his wickedness, and falling headlong, he burst open in the middle and all his intestines gushed out.

Answer: Neither Matthew nor Luke made a mistake. What you have is Matthew giving the reader the manner in which Judas committed suicide. On the other hand, Luke is giving the reader of Acts, the result of that suicide. Therefore, instead of a mistake, we have two texts that complement each other, really giving the reader the full picture. Judas came to a tree alongside a cliff that had rocks below. He tied the rope to a branch and the other end around his neck and jumped over the edge of the cliff in

---

[112] Meaning *face of God*

an attempt at hanging himself. One of two things could have happened: (1) the limb broke plunging him to the rocks below, or (2) the rope broke with the same result, and he burst open onto the rocks below.

Critic: The apostle Paul made a mistake when he quotes how many people died.

Numbers 25:9 Updated American Standard Version (UASV)

⁹ The ones who died in the plague were twenty-four thousand.

1 Corinthians 10:8 Updated American Standard Version (UASV)

⁸ Neither let us commit sexual immorality, as some of them committed sexual immorality, only to fall, twenty-three thousand of them in one day.

Answer: We must keep in mind the above principle that we spoke of, the *Intended Meaning of the Writer.* We live in a far more precise age today, where specificity is highly important. However, we round large numbers off (even estimate) all the time: "there were 237,000 people in Time Square last night." The simplest answer is that the number of people slain was in between 23,000 and 24,000, and both writers rounded the number off. However, there is even another possibility, because the book of Numbers specifically speaks of "all the chiefs of the people" (25:4-5), which could account for the extra 1,000, which is mentioned in Numbers 24,000. Thus, you have the people killing the chiefs of the people and the plague killing the people. Therefore, both books are correct.

Critic: After 215 years in Egypt, the descendants of Jacob arrived at the Promised Land. As you recall they sinned against God and were sentenced to forty years in the wilderness. But once they entered the Promised Land, they buried Joseph's bones "at Shechem, in the piece of land that *Jacob bought* from the sons of Hamor the father of Shechem," as stated at Joshua 24:32. Yet, when Stephen had to defend himself before the Jewish religious leaders, he said that Joseph was buried "in the tomb that *Abraham had bought* for a sum of silver from the sons of Hamor." Therefore, at once it appears that we have a mistake on the part of Stephen.

Acts 7:15-16 Updated American Standard Version (UASV)

¹⁵ And Jacob went down to Egypt and died, he and our fathers. ¹⁶ And they were brought back to Shechem and buried in the tomb that Abraham had bought for a sum of silver from the sons of Hamor in Shechem.

Genesis 23:17-18 Updated American Standard Version (UASV)

¹⁷ So Ephron's field, which was in Machpelah, which faced Mamre, the field and cave which was in it, and all the trees which were in the field, that were in all its border around, were made over ¹⁸ to Abraham for a

possession in the presence of the sons of Heth, before all who went in at the gate of his city.

Genesis 33:19 Updated American Standard Version (UASV)

[19] And he bought the piece of land where he had pitched his tent from the hand of the sons of Hamor, Shechem's father, for one hundred qesitahs.[113]

Joshua 24:32 Updated American Standard Version (UASV)

[32] As for the bones of Joseph, which the sons of Israel brought up from Egypt, they buried them at Shechem, in the piece of land that Jacob bought from the sons of Hamor the father of Shechem for one hundred qesitahs.[114] It became an inheritance of the sons of Joseph.

Answer: If we look back to Genesis 12:6-7, we will find that Abraham's first stop after entering Canaan from Haran was Shechem. It is here that Jehovah told Abraham: "To your offspring I will give this land." At this point Abraham built an altar to Jehovah. It seems reasonable that Abraham would need to purchase this land that had not yet been given to his offspring. While it is true that the Old Testament does not mention this purchase, it is likely that Stephen would be aware of such by way of oral tradition. As Acts chapter seven demonstrates, Stephen had a wide-ranging knowledge of Old Testament history.

Later, Jacob would have had difficulty laying claim to the tract of land that his grandfather Abraham had purchased, because there would have been a new generation of inhabitants of Shechem. This would have been many years after Abraham moved further south and Isaac moved to Beersheba, and including Jacob's twenty years in Paddan-aram (Gen 28:6, 7). The simplest answer is that this land was not in use for about 120 years because of Abraham's extensive travels and Isaac's having moved away, leaving it unused; likely it was put to use by others. So, Jacob simply repurchased what Abraham had bought over a hundred years earlier. This is very similar to the time Isaac had to repurchase the well at Beersheba that Abraham had already purchased earlier. – Genesis 21:27–30; 26:26–32.

Genesis 33:18–20 tells us that 'Jacob bought this land for a hundred pieces of money, from the sons of Hamor.' This same transaction is also mentioned at Joshua 24:32, in reference to transporting Joseph's bones from Egypt, to be buried in Shechem.

We should also address the cave of Machpelah that Abraham had purchased in Hebron from Ephron the Hittite. The word "tomb" is not mentioned until Joshua 24:32, and is in reference to the tract of land in

---

[113] Or *pieces of money*; money of unknown value
[114] Or *pieces of money*; money of unknown value

Shechem. Nowhere in the Old Testament does it say that Abraham bought a "tomb." The cave of Machpelah obtained by Abraham would eventually become a family tomb, receiving Sarah's body and, eventually, his own, and those of Isaac, Rebekah, Jacob, and Leah. (Genesis 23:14–19; 25:9; 49:30, 31; 50:13) Gleason L. Archer, Jr., concludes this Bible difficulty, saying:

> The reference to a *mnema* ("tomb") in connection with Shechem must either have been proleptic [to anticipate] for the later use of that shechemite tract for Joseph's tomb (i.e., 'the tomb that Abraham bought' was intended to imply 'the tomb location that Abraham bought"); or else conceivably the dative relative pronoun *ho* was intended elliptically [omission] for *en to topo ho onesato Abraam* ("in the place that Abraham bought") as describing the location of the *mnema* near the Oak of Moreh right outside Shechem. Normally Greek would have used the relative-locative adverb *hou* to express 'in which' or 'where'; but this would have left *onesato* ("bought") without an object in its own clause, and so *ho* was much more suitable in this context. (Archer 1982, 379–81)

Another solution could be that Jacob is being viewed as a representative of Abraham, for he is the grandson of Abraham. This was quite appropriate in Biblical times, to attribute the purchase to Abraham as the Patriarchal family head.

Critic: 2 Samuel 24:1 says that God moved David to count the Israelites, while 1 Chronicles 21:1 Satan, or a resister did. This would seem to be a clear mistake on the part of one of these authors.

2 Samuel 24:1 Updated American Standard Version (UASV)

¹ Now again the anger of Jehovah burned against Israel, and it incited David against them to say, "Go, number Israel and Judah."

1 Chronicles 21:1 Updated American Standard Version (UASV)

¹ Then Satan stood up against Israel and moved David to number Israel.

Answer: In this period of David's reign, Jehovah was very displeased with Israel, and therefore he did not prevent Satan from bringing this sin on them. Often in Scripture, it is spoken of as though God did something when he allowed an event to take place. For example, it is said that God 'hardened Pharaoh's heart' (Exodus 4:21), when he actually allowed the Pharaoh's heart to harden.

EDWARD D. ANDREWS

Inerrancy: Are There Scientific Errors?

Many truths about God are beyond the scope of science. Science and the Bible are not at odds. In fact, we can thank modern day science as it has helped us to better under the creation of God, from our solar system to the universes, to the human body and mind. What we find is a level of order, precision, design, and sophistication, which points to a Designer, the eyes of many Christians, to an Almighty God, with infinite intelligence and power. The apostle Paul makes this all too clear, when he writes, "For his invisible attributes, namely, his eternal power and divine nature, have been clearly perceived, ever since the creation of the world, in the things that have been made. So they are without excuse." – Romans 1:20.

Back in the seventeenth century, the world-renowned scientist Galileo proved beyond any doubt that the earth was not the center of the universe, nor did the sun orbit the earth. In fact, he proved it to be the other way around (no pun intended), with the earth revolving around the sun. However, he was brought up on charges of heresy by the Catholic Church and ordered to recant his position. Why? From the viewpoint of the Catholic Church, Galileo was contradicting God's Word, the Bible. As it turned out, Galileo and science were correct, and the Church was wrong, for which it issued a formal apology in 1992. However, the point we wish to make here is that in all the controversy, the Bible was never in the wrong. It was a misinterpretation on the part of the Catholic Church and not a fault with the Bible. One will find no place in the Bible that claims the sun orbits the earth. So where would the Church get such an idea? The Church got such an idea from Ptolemy (b. about 85 C.E.), an ancient astronomer, who argued for such an idea.

As it usually turns out, the so-called contradiction between science and God's Word lies at the feet of those who are interpreting Scripture incorrectly. To repeat the sentiments of Galileo when writing to a pupil–Galileo expressed the same sentiments: "Even though Scripture cannot err, its interpreters and expositors can, in various ways. One of these, very serious and very frequent, would be when they always want to stop at the purely literal sense."[115] I believe that today's scholars, in hindsight, would have no problem agreeing.

While the Bible is not a science textbook, it is scientifically accurate when it touches on matters of science.

The Circle of the Earth Hangs on Nothing

Isaiah 40:22 Updated American Standard Version (UASV)

---

[115] Letter from Galileo to Benedetto Castelli, December 21, 1613.

22 It is he who sits above **the circle of the earth,**
    and its inhabitants are like grasshoppers;
who stretches out the heavens like a curtain,
    and spreads them like a tent to dwell in.

More than 2,500 years ago, the prophet Isaiah wrote that the earth is a circle or sphere. First, how would it be possible for Isaiah to know the earth is a circle or sphere, if not from inspiration? Scientific America writes, "As countless photos from space can attest, Earth is round–the "Blue Marble," as astronauts have affectionately dubbed it. Appearances, however, can be deceiving. Planet Earth is not, in fact, perfectly round."[116] Scientifically speaking, the sun is not perfectly, absolutely 100 percent round but in everyday speech, this verse is both acceptable and accurate, when we keep in mind it is written from a human perspective, not from a scientific perspective. Moreover, Isaiah was not discussing astronomy; he was simply making an inspired observation that man came to realize once he was in space, looking back at the earth, it is round. See the section about title, "Intended Meaning of Writer."

Job 26:7 Updated American Standard Version (UASV)

7 "He stretches out the north over empty space
and hangs the earth on nothing.

Here the author describes the earth as hanging upon nothing. Many have never heard of the Greek mathematician and astronomer Eratosthenes. He was born in about 276 B.C.E. and received some of his education in Athens, Greece. In 240 B.C., the "Greek astronomer, geographer, mathematician and librarian Eratosthenes calculates the Earth's circumference. His data was rough, but he wasn't far off."[117] While man very early on used their God given intelligence to arrive at some outstanding conclusion that was actually very accurate, we learn two points here. Eratosthenes was a very astute scientist, while Isaiah, who wrote some 500 years earlier, was no scientist at all. Moreover, Moses, who wrote the book of Job over 1,230 years before Eratosthenes, knew that the earth hung upon nothing.

How Is the Sun Standing Still Possible?

Joshua 10:13 Updated American Standard Version (UASV)

---

116 Charles Q. Choi (April 12, 2007). Scientific America. Strange but True: Earth Is Not Round. Retrieved Monday, August 03, 2015.
http://www.scientificamerican.com/article/earth-is-not-round/
117 Alfred, Randy (June 19, 2008). "June 19, 240 B.C.E: The Earth Is Round, and It's This Big". Wired. Retrieved Monday, August 03, 2015.

¹³ And the sun stood still, and the moon stopped,
until the nation avenged themselves of their enemies.

Is this not written in the Book of Jashar? The sun stopped in the midst of heaven and did not hurry to set for about a whole day.

The Canaanites had besieged the Gibeonites, a group of people that gained Jehovah God's backing because they had faith in Him. In this battle, Jehovah helped the Israelites continue their attack by causing "the sun [to stand] still, and the moon stopped, until the nation took vengeance on their enemies." (Jos 10:1-14) Those who accept God as the creator of the universe and life can accept that he would know a way of stopping the earth from rotating. However, there are other ways of understanding this account. We must keep in mind that the Bible speaks from an earthly observer point of view, so it need not be that he stopped the rotation. It could have been a refraction of solar and lunar light rays, which would have produced the same effect.

Psalm 136:6 Updated American Standard Version (UASV)

⁶ to him who spread out the earth above the waters,
for his lovingkindness is everlasting;

Hebrews 3:4 Updated American Standard Version (UASV)

⁴ For every house is built by someone, but the builder of all things is God.

2 Kings 20:8-11 Updated American Standard Version (UASV)

⁸ And Hezekiah said to Isaiah, "What shall be the sign that Jehovah will heal me, and that I shall go up to the house of Jehovah on the third day?" ⁹ And Isaiah said, "This shall be the sign to you from Jehovah, that Jehovah will do the thing that he has spoken: shall the shadow go forward ten steps or go back ten steps?" ¹⁰ And Hezekiah answered, "It is an easy thing for the shadow to decline ten steps; no, but let the shadow turn backward ten steps." ¹¹ And Isaiah the prophet cried to Jehovah, and he brought the shadow on the steps back ten steps, by which it had gone down on the steps of Ahaz.

How is it that the stars fought on behalf of Barak?

Judges 5:20 Updated American Standard Version (UASV)

²⁰ From heaven the stars fought, from their courses they fought against Sisera.

Judges 4:15 Updated American Standard Version (UASV)

[15] And Jehovah routed Sisera and all his chariots and all his army with the edge of the sword before Barak; and Sisera alighted from his chariot and fled away on foot.

In the Bible, you have Biblical prose, and Biblical poetry.

Prose: language that is not poetry: (1) writing or speech in its normal continuous form, without the rhythmic or visual line structure of poetry **(2)** ordinary style of expression: writing or speech that is ordinary or matter-of-fact, without embellishment.

Poetry: literature in verse: (1) literary works written in verse, in particular verse writing of high quality, great beauty, emotional sincerity or intensity, or profound insight **(2) beauty or grace:** something that resembles poetry in its beauty, rhythmic grace, or imaginative, elevated, or decorative style.

We have a beautiful example of both of these forms of writing communication in chapters four and five of the book of Judges. Judges, Chapter 4 is a prose account of Deborah and Barak, while Judges Chapter 5 is a poetic account. As we have learned from the above, poetry is less concerned with accuracy than evoking emotions. Poetry has a license to say things like what we find in of 5:20, which is in the poetry chapter: "from heaven the stars fought." This can be said, and the reader is expected not to take the language literally. What we can surmise from it though, is that God was acting against Sisera in some way, there was divine intervention.

Procedures for Handling Biblical Difficulties

1. You need to be completely convinced a reason or understanding exists.

2. You need to have total trust and conviction in the inerrancy of the Scripture as originally written down.

3. You need to study the context and framework of the verse carefully, to establish what the author meant by the words he used. In other words, find the beginning and the end of the context that your passage falls within.

4. You need to understand exegesis: find the historical setting, determine author intent, study key words, and note parallel passages. You need to slow down and carefully read the account, considering exactly what is being said

5. You need to find a reasonable harmonization of parallel passages.

6. You need to consider a variety of trusted Bible commentaries, dictionaries, lexical sources, encyclopedias, as well as books on Bible difficulties.

7. You should investigate as to whether the difficulty is a transmission error in the original text.

8. You must always keep in mind that the historical accuracy of the biblical text is unmatched; that thousands of extant manuscripts some of which date back to the second century B.C. support the transmitted text of Scripture.

9. We must keep in mind that the Bible is a diverse book when it comes to literary styles: narrative, poetic, prophetic, and apocalyptic; also containing parables, metaphors, similes, hyperbole, and other figures of speech. Too often, these alleged errors are the result of a reader taking a figure of speech as literal or reading a parable as though it is a narrative.

10. The Bible student needs to understand what level that the Bible intends to be exact in what is written. If Jim told a friend that 650 graduated with him from high school in 1984, it is not challenged, because it is all too clear that he is using rounded numbers and is not meaning to be precise.

Bibliography

Archer, G. L. (1982). *New International Encyclopedia of Bible Difficulties, Zondervan's Understand the Bible Reference Series.* Zondervan Publishing House: Grand Rapids, MI.

Boice, J. M. (1986). *Foundations of the Christian Faith.* Downers Grove, IL: IVP Academic.

Brand, C., Draper, C., & Archie, E. (2003). *Holman Illustrated Bible Dictionary: Revised, Updated and Expanded.* Nashville, TN: Holman.

Bromiley, G. W. (1986). *The International Standard Bible Encyclopedia (Vol. 1-4).* Grand Rapids, MI: William B. Eerdmans Publishing Co.

Bromiley, G. W., & Friedrich, G. (1964-). *Theological Dictionary of the New Testament, ed. Gerhard Kittel, vol. 4.* Grand Rapids, MI: Eerdmans.

Caba, T. e. (2007). *The Apologetics Study Bible: Real Questions, Straight Answers, Stronger Faith.* Nashville: Holman Bible Publishers.

Elwell, W. A. (2001). *Evangelical Dictionary of Theology (Second Edition).* Grand Rapids: Baker Academic.

Elwell, W. A., & Beitzel, B. J. (1988). *Baker Encyclopedia of the Bible.* Grand Rapids, MI: Baker Book House.

Elwell, W. A., & Comfort, P. W. (2001). *Tyndale Bible Dictionary.* Wheaton: Tyndale House Publishers.

Exell, J. S., & Leale, T. H. (1892). *Genesis, The Preacher's Complete Homiletic Commentary.* New York; London; Toronto: Funk & Wagnalls Company.

Geisler, N. L., & Nix, W. E. (1996). *A General Introduction to the Bible.* Chicago: Moody Press.

Hendriksen, W., & Kistemaker, S. J. (1953-2001). *Exposition of the Pastoral Epistles, New Testament Commentary vol. 4,.* Grand Rapid: Baker Book House.

Howe, T., & L., G. N. (1992). *BIG BOOK OF BIBLE DIFFICULTIES, The: Clear and Concise Answers from Genesis to Revelation.* Grand Rapids, MI: Baker Books.

Kistemaker, S. J. (1984). *Baker New Testament Commentary: Hebrews.* Grand Rapids: Baker Books.

Lea, T. D. (1999). *Holman New Testament Commentary: Hebrews, James.* Nashville, TN: Broadman & Holman Publishers.

Mathews, K. A. (2001). *The New American Commentary vol. 1A, Genesis 1-11:26 .* Nashville: Broadman & Holman Publishers.

Matthews, K. A. (2001). *The New American Commentary Vol. 1B, Genesis 11:27-50:26.* Nashville: Broadman and Holman Publishers.

Mounce, W. D. (2006). *Mounce's Complete Expository Dictionary of Old & New Testament Words.* Grand Rapids, MI: Zondervan.

Smith, W. (1890). *Smith's Dictionary of the Bible.* New York, NY: Hurd and Houghton, Cambridge Riverside Press.

Sproul, R. C. (2010). *What Is Faith?* Lake Mary: Reformation Trust.

Swanson, J. (1997). *Dictionary of Biblical Languages with Semantic Domains: Greek (New Testament).* Oak Harbor: Logos Research Systems.

Swanson, J. (1997). *Dictionary of Biblical Languages with Semantic Domains: Hebrew (Old Testament).* Oak Harbor: Logos Research Systems.

Tremper, L. I. (2005). *How to Read Genesis (How to Read Series How to Read).* Grand Rapids: Intervarsity Press.

Vunderink, R. W., & Bromiley, G. W. (1979–1988). *The International Standard Bible Encyclopedia, Revised (, .* Grand Rapids, MI: Wm. B. Eerdmans.

Wood, D. R. (1996). *New Bible Dictionary (Third Edition).* Downers Grove: InterVarsity Press.

Zodhiates, S. (2000, c1992, c1993). *The Complete Word Study Dictionary: New Testament.* Chattanooga: AMG Publishers.

www.ingramcontent.com/pod-product-compliance
Lightning Source LLC
Chambersburg PA
CBHW070114070426
42448CB00039B/2785